FIFTY-FIFTY

A speaking and listening course

INTRO

Third Edition

PEARSON
Longman

WARREN WILSON • ROGER BARNARD

Published by
Longman Asia ELT
2/F Cornwall House
Taikoo Place
979 King's Road
Quarry Bay
Hong Kong

fax: +852 2856 9578
email: pearsonlongman@pearsoned.com.hk
www.longman.com

and Associated Companies throughout the world.

First edition 1998
This edition 2007

Produced by Pearson Education Asia Limited, Hong Kong
GCC/01

ISBN-13: 978-962-00-5664-2
ISBN-10: 962-00-5664-7

Publisher: Rachel Wilson
Editor: Mark Horsley
Designers: Junko Funaki, Angel Chan
Illustrators: Roger Barnard, Megan Cash, Andrew Lange, Teddy Wong

Acknowledgments

We would like to thank the following reviewers for the insightful feedback
provided for this edition: Yu-Ping Chang, Pei-Ling (Bessie) Chuang, Patrick
Davis, John Doodigian, William Figoni, Daniel Gossman, Jennifer Hickey,
Christopher Kerr, Kitai Kim, Carmella Lieske, Moon-Jeong Lim, John
Matthews, Michael S. Neiburg, Hugh Palmer, Trafford Parry, Caleb Prichard,
Andrew Reinmann, Richard H. Schaepe, Mike Shearer, Kenji Takahashi,
Marissa Troxell and David Whitmore.

CONTENTS

Acknowledgments

We would like to thank the teachers and students at the following schools for their valuable help in developing and revising this material:

- Athénée-Français, Tokyo
- Community English Program, Teachers College, Columbia University, New York
- Cosmopolitan Language Institute, Tokyo
- English Language Institute, Queens College, New York
- Haggerty English Language Program, SUNY New Paltz, New York
- International English Language Institute, Hunter College, New York
- Tama Art University, Tokyo
- Tokyo School of Business, Tokyo

We would also like to thank those at Prentice Hall who worked on this project originally, particularly our first production editor, Noël Vreeland Carter. For this new edition, we owe much to our publisher, Rachel Wilson, our editor, Mark Horsley, our design manager, Winnie Sung, and her team of talented designers including Junko Funaki, Tonic Ng and Angel Chan, and all the great people at Pearson Longman.

For Masako, Sophie, In Sook, Mia and Dale.

R.B.
W.W.
Tokyo / New York
September 2006

INTRODUCTION

Fifty-Fifty Third Edition is a three-level course in communicative English that provides listening and speaking practice for students from the elementary level through the intermediate level. Designed primarily for use in large classes where "student talking" time is usually very limited, this material can be used effectively in virtually any size class since students actively participate in meaningful exchanges during pair work and group work. The focus is on listening and speaking proficiency. *Fifty-Fifty* Third Edition provides realistic yet manageable listening tasks, and extended pair work and group work tasks, all of which are designed to reduce learner anxiety and promote language acquisition via student participation in purposeful interaction.

Fifty-Fifty Intro is for students at the elementary level who may have some passive knowledge of grammar and vocabulary from previous study, but lack the skills and confidence to participate in conversation. The text consists of a warm-up unit, twelve main units and three review units. The *Appendix* contains the *Student B pages* of the pair work and group work activities, the *Self-study exercises* with *Answer key* for out-of-class review and the *Audio script* for the *Listening tasks*.

Each unit consists of the following sections. (The format of the review units differs slightly.)

● Warm-up exercises

Each unit begins with some simple warm-up exercises. *Exercise 1* is in the form of a comic sketch. The sketch has a question or an answer to be written by the student. The sketch illustrates the unit theme and introduces, in a simple context, the language to be practiced.

Exercise 2 and *Exercise 3* center on a dialogue that functions as a model that the students can listen to and practice reading through with a partner. The dialogue can also be used for freer conversation practice in which the students supply their own information.

● Listening task

The *Listening task* helps the students focus on the particular language points to be practiced. The students are not expected to retain or reproduce *all* the language they hear on the recording, but their aural comprehension of the target structures and vocabulary will increase as they listen for the information needed to complete the task.

It is suggested that the students listen several times: once to familiarize the students with the content, then again with pauses as the students complete the task and once more straight through as they check their answers. After the teacher has elicited the answers, the students could listen a final time, perhaps while going over the audio script. The *Audio script* for the *Listening task* is located in the *Appendix* and can also be used for extended practice and/or review of grammar and vocabulary. The *Teacher's Edition* provides helpful hints, as well as the answers, to ensure that the exercise goes smoothly.

● Speaking task one

Speaking task one provides communicative practice that maximizes "student talking" time. Students complete the task by asking partners for missing information. Being task-based, the exercise provides more than just question-and-answer practice: genuine communication takes place. The completion of each task relies on actual information sharing and feedback between students conversing in pairs.

It is suggested that the teacher try having students sit face to face, if possible, and maintain eye contact while speaking. They should avoid looking at each other's pages and should always ask for spelling or repetition in English. It is advisable to circulate once quickly at the outset to make sure that each student understands what to do and gets off to a good start. Correction techniques vary from teacher to teacher and exercise to exercise; however, during communicative practice it is usually advisable to leave most correction until afterward. The point of the tasks is communication, not the production of flawless sentences. (Nevertheless, errors that interfere with comprehension and/or are counterproductive to the practice should be rectified appropriately.)

Finally, the teacher can check the finished work by scanning students' pages and briefly querying their partners to verify answers. Students can also confer and compare answers themselves.

Speaking task two

Speaking task two is generally a bit "freer" than *Speaking task one* and is meant to provide additional practice in a slightly different context. *Speaking task two* exercises include "Find someone who" activities, group interviews and various types of language games that promote interaction while lessening learner anxiety.

All suggestions given above for *Speaking task one* apply to this section; the recommended procedures are the same.

Language game

In the review units, *Speaking task two* is followed by a section labeled *Language game*, an activity that encourages focused listening. The point of the game is to provide ample comprehensible input containing vocabulary and structures from the preceding units, as well as pronunciation practice—hopefully more in an atmosphere of fun, and less of conscious language study.

Homework

The last page of each main unit contains the *Homework* section, which is a brief writing assignment that students must do on a separate sheet of paper to be handed in. The *Homework* section includes a *Homework review* exercise, an optional follow-up exercise for in-class use, time permitting. Please note that some of these exercises might require the teacher's correction of the students' written homework before it is used as an oral/aural activity in class.

Language focus

The *Language focus* section at the end of each main unit contains an overview of the sentence structures presented in the unit, providing language models for the students that they can use for a quick reference while doing the exercises.

Student B pages

Student A, turn to page 4

This section in the *Appendix* contains all the pages necessary for the information gap activities, when students working in pairs or small groups must look at different pages. In the units, these activities contain a page reference in the upper right-hand corner. It might be a good idea to remind students not to look at their partner's pages or to flip back and forth between the *Student A* and *Student B pages*.

Self-study exercises and Answer key

The *Self-study exercises* in the *Appendix* review and consolidate material covered in the twelve main units, providing students with added listening practice through recycling some of the *Listening task* audio. The accompanying *Answer key* provides all of the answers to the *Self-study exercises* and enables students to assess their own performance and their progress towards aural mastery of the listening material. Students can download the *Self-study Audio* by visiting the *Fifty-Fifty* website at www.fifty-fifty-series.com

Audio script

The *Audio script* in the *Appendix* contains the *Listening task* material. The introductory dialogue in the *Warm-up exercises* of each unit is not included in the *Audio script* since the dialogue itself serves as the script.

In addition to the Student Book, the *Fifty-Fifty* series includes the following components:
- Teacher's Edition with Test Master CD-ROM Pack
- Class CD
- Companion Website: www.fifty-fifty-series.com
- Downloadable: Self-study Audio
- Downloadable: Class Audio

The authors hope you and your students enjoy using *Fifty-Fifty* Third Edition and would appreciate any comments or suggestions you might have. They can be contacted via the *Fifty-Fifty* website.

GETTING STARTED
Introductory exercises

Warm-up exercises

Exercise 1

Write the girl's answers.

Are you in this class?

Do you know the teacher's name?

Exercise 2 1

Listen to the following conversation. Then practice it with a partner.

Jimmy	Hi, Denise. Am I late?
Denise	No, you're not late. Class starts in five minutes.
Jimmy	Do you have the homework?
Denise	Yes, I do.
Jimmy	Well, I don't. Does Mr. Lee want it today?
Denise	Yes, he does.

Exercise 3

Practice the conversation again. This time, Denise cannot look at the page.

Look at page 5
Language focus

2

Listening task

Exercise 1 2

Listen to the questions (1–8) and write the number of the question on the correct answer.

☐ Yes, he is.

☐ No, it isn't.

☐ It's over there, on the right.

☐ Yes, I am.

☐ No, I don't.

☐ Yes, we are.

☐ They're in the classroom.

☐ It starts at 9:00.

Exercise 2 3

Read the questions below and then listen to the conversation with your *book closed*. Open your book and check (✓) "Yes" or "No" for each question. Listen again (with your book open) and check your answers.

		Yes	No
1	Is the boy a new student?	☐	☐
2	Are the boy and girl in the same reading class?	☐	☐
3	Do they like reading?	☐	☐
4	Does the boy live in Hillside?	☐	☐
5	Do the boy and girl live in the same town?	☐	☐
6	Is the girl's home near the school?	☐	☐
7	Does the girl walk to school?	☐	☐
8	Does the boy walk to school?	☐	☐
9	Are they in the same writing class in the afternoon?	☐	☐
10	Is the writing class easy?	☐	☐

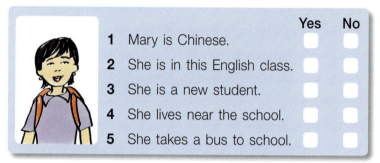
Speaking task one

Exercise 1

Look at each sentence (1–5) and make a yes/no question. Ask Student B each question and check (✓) "Yes" or "No."

Memo

Ask *only* yes/no questions.

Example

Student A	Is Mary Chinese?
Student B	Yes, she is.
Student A	Does she live near the school?
Student B	No, she doesn't.

		Yes	No
1	Mary is Chinese.	☐	☐
2	She is in this English class.	☐	☐
3	She is a new student.	☐	☐
4	She lives near the school.	☐	☐
5	She takes a bus to school.	☐	☐

Exercise 2

Read the sentences about Carlos and answer Student B's questions.

Memo

Answer in *short* sentences.

Example

Student B	Is Carlos Mexican?
Student A	No, he isn't.
Student B	Does he live near the school?
Student A	Yes, he does.

Carlos is Brazilian. He is not in this English class. He is a new student. He lives near the school. He does not take a bus to school. He walks to school.

Speaking task two Do this exercise with everyone.

The teacher will give you one of the boxes (1–4) below. Walk around the classroom and talk to your classmates. Ask a yes/no question for each sentence. If the answer is "yes," write the person's name in the blank.

Vocabulary

- far
- apartment
- finished
- city
- very
- exercise

Example

Student A	Are you a new student?	**Student B**	Do you take a bus to school?
Student B	No, I'm not.	**Student C**	Yes, I do.

1 Find someone who:

_____ is a new student.
name

_____ lives near the school.
name

_____ lives in the city.
name

_____ does *not* walk to school.
name

2 Find someone who:

_____ walks to school.
name

_____ lives in a house.
name

_____ does *not* live near the school.
name

_____ is *not* a new student.
name

3 Find someone who:

_____ takes a bus to school.
name

_____ lives very far from the school.
name

_____ lives in an apartment.
name

_____ does *not* live in the city.
name

4 Find someone who:

_____ comes to school by car.
name

_____ does *not* take a bus to school.
name

_____ does *not* live far from the school.
name

_____ is finished with this exercise.
name

Language focus

Are	you / they	in this class?			Yes,	I	am.	No,	I'm	not.
	he / she					he / she / it	is.		he / she / it	isn't.
Is	it	a large class?				we / they	are.		we / they	aren't.

Do	you / they	walk to school?			Yes,	I / we / they	do.	No,	I / we / they	don't.
Does	he / she					he / she	does.		he / she	doesn't.

5

Warm-up exercises

Exercise 1

Write the police officer's question.

Exercise 2 4

Listen to the following conversation. Then practice it with a partner.

> **Memo**
>
> Always look at the person you are speaking to. Don't look down at the page!

Mr. Ames	Could I have your student ID number, please?
Robert	Yes, it's 184-73-9650.
Mr. Ames	OK. Could you tell me your name?
Robert	Robert Zimmerman.
Mr. Ames	How do you spell "Zimmerman"?
Robert	Z-I-M-M-E-R-M-A-N.

Exercise 3

Practice the conversation again. This time, Robert cannot look at the page. Answer the questions with *true* information or make up the answers.

Look at page 10
Language focus

Listening task

Exercise 1 5–7

Write the number of each conversation (1–3) next to the correct picture.

Memo

There are conversations for *only* three pictures.

Exercise 2 5–7

Listen to the conversations again and fill in the correct information.

Vocabulary

- last name
- business
- area code
- corner
- social security number
- misdial

1	(a) The address of the place is	
	(b) The name of the place is	
2	(a) The woman's phone number is	
	(b) The woman's area code is	
3	(a) The girl's last name is	
	(b) Her social security number is	

Speaking task one Do Exercise 1 alone and Exercise 2 with different partners.

Exercise 1

Write down your name, address, telephone number and email address in the box on the right. (You can use *true* information or you can make up the information.)

Your information:

Name:

Address:

Tel. No.:

Email:

Exercise 2

Walk around the classroom and talk to your classmates. Write down the name, address, telephone number and email address of one classmate in each box below.

Memo

Talk in *pairs*, not in groups.

Classmate 1:

Name:

Address:

Tel. No.:

Email:

Example

Student A	Could I have your name, please?
Student B	John Doe.
Student A	How do you spell "Doe"?
Student B	D-O-E.
Student A	Could you tell me your address?
Student B	Sure, it's 50 Main Street, Oakdale, New York.

Classmate 2:

Name:

Address:

Tel. No.:

Email:

Classmate 3:

Name:

Address:

Tel. No.:

Email:

Caller, turn to page 87

Language game   Play this game with two to four "players" and one "caller."

Take turns choosing two numbers (1–16) from the grid below. Each number is a question or an answer. The caller will read each sentence that you choose.

Choose one number, listen to the caller read the sentence and then choose another number. Try to match a question with the answer. Do not write any notes. Just listen!

Continue until all the questions and answers have been matched. The player with the most matches wins!

Memo

- Cross off (✗) all matched numbers and circle your matches.
- Look at this page only!
- The teacher may let you write notes on the numbers.

Example

Player A	Number 4.	Player B	Number 16.
Caller	"Could I have your address?"	Caller	"Yes, it's 36 Main Street, Dover."
Player A	Number 11.	Player B	Number 4.
Caller	"Yes, I do." They don't match!	Caller	"Could I have your address?" They match!

1	2	3	4
5	6	7	8
9	10	11	12
13	14	15	16

Homework

Choose one city or country from each of the six continents below. Fill in each blank.

Memo

Look at a map to find cities or countries.

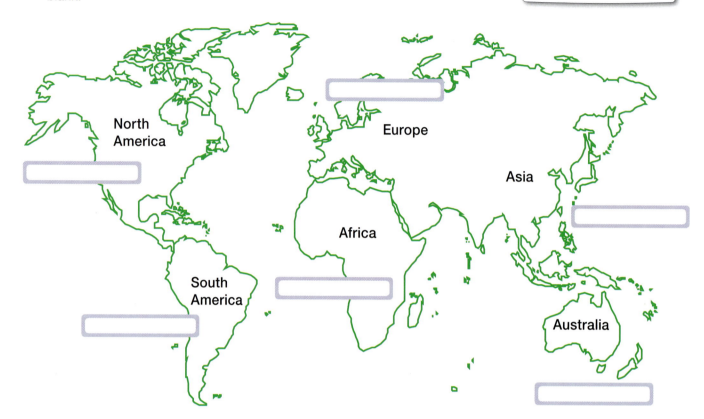

Homework review   Work in a group of three.

Student A
Ask your partners to spell the name of each city or country you wrote for homework.

Students B and C
Take turns and try to spell the name of each city or country that Student A tells you (with your *book closed*).

Memo

• Do this exercise in the next lesson if you have time.

• Each time take a turn as Student A.

Example

Student A   How do you spell "China"?
Student B   C-H-I-N-A.

Language focus

| Could you tell me | your | phone number? | | Sure, | (it's) | 555-1093. |
| Could I have | | name? | → | Yes, | | Pat Wei. |

How do you spell	that?		W-E-I.
	your last name?	→	
	"Wei"?		

Warm-up exercises

Exercise 1

Write the woman's questions.

Exercise 2 8

Listen to the following conversation. Then practice it with a partner.

Maria	Sapporo is a beautiful place. Do you live here?
Carmelo	No, I live in Tokyo.
Maria	Oh, really? Where are you from?
Carmelo	I'm from Italy.
Maria	Oh, I see. So, what languages do you speak?
Carmelo	I speak Italian, Japanese and English.

Memo

Always look at the person you are speaking to. Don't look down at the page!

Exercise 3

Practice the conversation again. This time, Carmelo cannot look at the page. Answer the questions with *true* information or make up the answers.

Look at page 16

Language focus

11

Listening task

Exercise 1 9–11

Listen and fill in each blank with the correct country, city or language. (Listen carefully: they are in a *different* order each time!)

Vocabulary

COUNTRIES	CITIES	LANGUAGES
• Denmark • Korea	• New Delhi • Rio de Janeiro	• Korean • French
• Switzerland • Brazil	• Seoul • Copenhagen	• Portuguese • Danish
• India	• Geneva	• Hindi

1   Meena

She is from ....

She lives in ....

She speaks ....

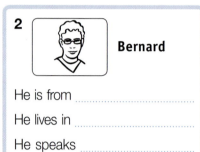

2   Bernard

He is from ....

He lives in ....

He speaks ....

3   Roberto and Paola

They are from ....

They live in ....

They speak ....

Exercise 2 12

Listen to the conversation and check (✓) all the correct information for the woman and the man.

The woman   The man

☐ ☐   is from Spain.
☐ ☐   is from Taiwan.
☐ ☐   is from Ecuador.
☐ ☐   lives in the countryside.
☐ ☐   lives in the suburbs.
☐ ☐   lives in the city.
☐ ☐   speaks Spanish.
☐ ☐   speaks Italian.
☐ ☐   speaks Chinese.

Exercise 3

Work with a partner and ask each other yes/no questions about the man and woman. (Answer with your *book closed*.)

Memo

Take turns asking and answering questions.

Example

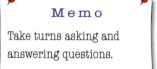

Student A	Is the woman from Spain?	**Student B**	Does the man live in the city?
Student B	No, she isn't.	**Student A**	Yes, he does.

Student B, turn to page 88

Speaking task one

Exercise 1

Ask Student B questions about the four people below and fill in the information in the boxes below for each one (1–4).

Example

Student A Could I have her name?	**Student A** Where's she from?
Student B Her name's Eri Park.	**Student B** She's from Korea.

1 Personal information:

Name: ....

Country: ....

Languages: ....

....

Lives in: ....

2 Personal information:

Name: ....

Country: ....

Languages: ....

....

Lives in: ....

3 Personal information:

Name: ....

Country: ....

Languages: ....

....

Lives in: ....

4 Personal information:

Name: ....

Country: ....

Languages: ....

....

Lives in: ....

Exercise 2

Ask Student B questions and fill in the information about Student B in the box below.

Memo

Change roles as Student A and Student B, and do the exercises again.

Personal information:

Name: ....

Country: ....

Languages: ....

....

Lives in: ....

Example

Student A Could I have your name?
Student B My name's Maria Ramirez.
Student A Where are you from?
Student B I'm from Mexico.

Speaking task two Do this exercise with everyone.

The teacher will give you *one* of the boxes (1–8) on pages 14 and 15. Walk around and talk to your classmates.

Ask yes/no questions and write one person's name in each blank.

Use this information to answer questions.

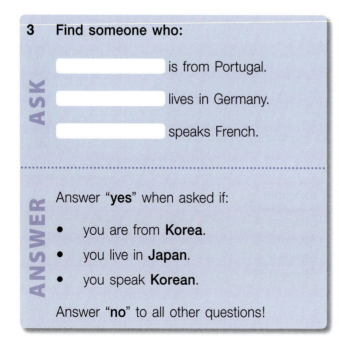

1 Find someone who:

ASK

[_____] is from Morocco.

[_____] lives in Italy.

[_____] speaks Korean.

ANSWER

Answer "**yes**" when asked if:

- you are from **Spain**.
- you live in **Germany**.
- you speak **Spanish**.

Answer "**no**" to all other questions!

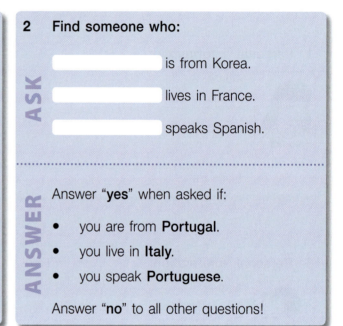

2 Find someone who:

ASK

[_____] is from Korea.

[_____] lives in France.

[_____] speaks Spanish.

ANSWER

Answer "**yes**" when asked if:

- you are from **Portugal**.
- you live in **Italy**.
- you speak **Portuguese**.

Answer "**no**" to all other questions!

3 Find someone who:

ASK

[_____] is from Portugal.

[_____] lives in Germany.

[_____] speaks French.

ANSWER

Answer "**yes**" when asked if:

- you are from **Korea**.
- you live in **Japan**.
- you speak **Korean**.

Answer "**no**" to all other questions!

4 Find someone who:

ASK

[_____] is from Spain.

[_____] lives in Japan.

[_____] speaks Portuguese.

ANSWER

Answer "**yes**" when asked if:

- you are from **Morocco**.
- you live in **France**.
- you speak **French**.

Answer "**no**" to all other questions!

Example

Student A	Are you from Spain?	Student C	Do you live in Italy?
Student B	Yes, I am.	Student D	Yes, I do.
Student B	Are you from Morocco?	Student D	Do you speak Spanish?
Student C	No, I'm not.	Student E	No, I don't.

M e m o
- Don't show your box to anyone!
- Talk in pairs, not groups.

---

5 Find someone who:

ASK

_____ is from Greece.

_____ lives in Canada.

_____ speaks Malay.

ANSWER

Answer "**yes**" when asked if:

- you are from **the Netherlands**.
- you live in **London**.
- you speak **Dutch**.

Answer "**no**" to all other questions!

---

6 Find someone who:

ASK

_____ is from Singapore.

_____ lives in Australia.

_____ speaks Dutch.

ANSWER

Answer "**yes**" when asked if:

- you are from **Hong Kong**.
- you live in **Canada**.
- you speak **Chinese**.

Answer "**no**" to all other questions!

---

7 Find someone who:

ASK

_____ is from Hong Kong.

_____ lives in London.

_____ speaks Greek.

ANSWER

Answer "**yes**" when asked if:

- you are from **Singapore**.
- you live in **New York**.
- you speak **Malay**.

Answer "**no**" to all other questions!

---

8 Find someone who:

ASK

_____ is from the Netherlands.

_____ lives in New York.

_____ speaks Chinese.

ANSWER

Answer "**yes**" when asked if:

- you are from **Greece**.
- you live in **Australia**.
- you speak **Greek**.

Answer "**no**" to all other questions!

Homework

Choose countries for the people below and draw lines from the people to the countries. Write the name of the country on the map and write three sentences for each one: **(1)** country, **(2)** nationality and **(3)** language.

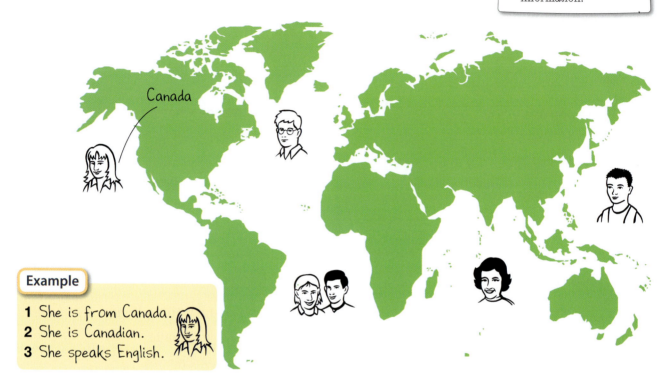

Example

1 She is from Canada.
2 She is Canadian.
3 She speaks English.

Homework review   **Work in a group of three or four students.**

Student A
Tell your partners one of your sentences you wrote for homework for each person (the country, nationality or language).

Students B, C and D
Take turns and try to guess the other two sentences that Student A wrote (the country, nationality or language).

Language focus

| Where | do | you / they | live? | → | I / We / They | live | in | New York. |
| | does | he / she | | | He / She | lives | | Boston. |

Where	are	you / they	from?	→	I'm		from	France.
	is	he / she			He's / She's			India.
					We're / They're			Japan.

What nationality	are	you / they?		→	I'm			French.
	is	he / she?			He's / She's			Indian.
					We're / They're			Japanese.

| What language(s) | do | you / they | speak? | → | I / We / They | speak | French. |
| | does | he / she | | | He / She | speaks | Hindi and Urdu. |

Warm-up exercises

Exercise 1

Write the father's answers.

Exercise 2 13

Listen to the following conversation. Then practice it with a partner.

Memo

Always look at the person you are speaking to. Don't look down at the page!

Alan	OK, are you in the study?
Sophie	Yes, I am.
Alan	Is my briefcase on the floor, next to the desk?
Sophie	Yes, it is.
Alan	Is my wallet in the briefcase?
Sophie	Wait a minute. No, it isn't. Your wallet isn't here.

Exercise 3

Practice the conversation again. This time, Sophie cannot look at the page. Answer the questions with the same information or make up the answers.

Look at page 22

Language focus

17

Listening task

Exercise 1 14

Listen to sentences 1 to 10 about objects in the office and circle the objects in the picture that are mentioned.

Vocabulary

LOCATIONS

- in
- in front of
- on
- next to
- under
- between
- over
- on the right/left
- behind
- in the middle of

OBJECTS

- file cabinet
- calendar
- CD player
- fish tank
- calculator
- scissors
- fax machine
- clock
- window
- briefcase
- keys
- watch
- camera
- lamp
- weights

Exercise 2 15

Listen to ten more sentences and write the number of the sentence (1–10) on each object.

Exercise 3 16

Listen and circle "true" or "false" for each sentence.

1	true	false	**2**	true	false	**3**	true	false	**4**	true	false	**5**	true	false
6	true	false	**7**	true	false	**8**	true	false	**9**	true	false	**10**	true	false

Student B, turn to page 89

Speaking task one

The picture below is different from Student B's picture. Ask and answer questions about the people and things in the picture, and circle anything in a different location.

Memo

• Don't look at Student B's picture.

• You can also ask, "Where is the ... ?" or "Where are the ... ?"

Example			
Student A	Is the canoe next to the pond?	**Student B**	Are the sleeping bags in the tent?
Student B	Yes, it is.	**Student A**	No, they aren't.

Vocabulary				
• canoe	• pond	• ground	• rock	• cows
• fish	• squirrel	• branch	• grill	• cooler
• tent	• sleeping bags	• firewood	• picnic table	• ax

19

Speaking task two

Exercise 1

Ask Student B for the location of the people and objects below (1–8), and write the numbers in the correct places on the picture (pages 20 and 21).

Example

| Student A | Where's the letter carrier? |
| Student B | He's in front of the post office, next to the door, on the right. |

Memo

- Don't look at Student B's book!
- You can also make a simple drawing of the people and objects in the picture.

1 letter carrier
2 pay phones
3 taxi cab
4 children
5 lamp posts
6 cat
7 ice cream truck
8 trash cans

Student B, turn to pages 90–91

Exercise 2

Listen to Student B's questions about the location of the people and objects in the picture below (pages 20 and 21), and tell Student B where each one is.

Example

Student B	Where are the mailboxes?
Student A	They're in front of the post office, next to the door, on the left.

Vocabulary

- bicycle
- mailboxes
- bus
- motorcycle

- construction workers
- police officer
- dogs
- traffic lights

- corner
- playground
- crosswalk
- roof

- lot
- sidewalk
- park
- street

21

Homework

Write the police officer's question and the thief's answer for each item (1–8).

Memo

Write the questions and answers on a separate sheet of paper.

Homework review Do this exercise with everyone.

Walk around and talk to your classmates. Ask and answer questions about the items (1–8) above. For each item, find someone who wrote the same answer as you and write that person's name next to your sentence.

Memo

• Do this exercise in the next lesson if you have time.

• If you cannot find anyone, write "no one."

Language focus

Is the bag	in front of				it is.		it isn't.
Is the woman	behind	the desk?	→	Yes,	she is.	No,	she isn't.
Are my shoes	under				they are.		they aren't.

	is	the briefcase?		It's	in	
Where		the police officer?	→	He's	next to	the police car.
	are	the sunglasses?		They're	on	

The TV remote control	is	in the living room, on the table.
The children	are	in the playground.
The fur coats		in the wardrobe.

4 DOING THINGS
Actions

Warm-up exercises

Exercise 1

Write the man's answers.

What's John doing?

What's Mary doing?

What are you doing?

SPORTS

Exercise 2 17

Listen to the following conversation. Then practice it with a partner.

> **Memo**
> Always look at the person you are speaking to. Don't look down at the page!

Angie	What are you watching?
Billy	A soccer game. Italy is playing Korea.
Angie	Where are they playing?
Billy	They're playing in Seoul.
Angie	Who's winning?
Billy	Korea is, 2-1.

Exercise 3

Practice the conversation again. This time, Billy cannot look at the page. Answer the questions with the same information or make up the answers.

Look at page 27
Language focus

23

Listening task

Exercise 1 18

Listen to Susan talking to her husband, Paul, on the telephone. Match the names (1–9) below with the people in the picture.

1	Megan	**2**	Erica	**3**	Nicky
4	Bob	**5**	Mary	**6**	Paul's mother
7	Paul's father	**8**	Susan's mother	**9**	Jimmy

Memo

You can draw lines or write numbers to match the names.

Vocabulary

- play
- change
- yell
- feed
- break
- take a nap
- noise
- basketball
- armchair
- light bulb
- couch
- movie

Exercise 2 19

Listen and circle "true" or "false" for each sentence.

1	true	false	**2**	true	false	**3**	true	false	**4**	true	false
5	true	false	**6**	true	false	**7**	true	false	**8**	true	false

Speaking task one

The picture of the park scene below is a little different from Student B's picture. Talk about the people's actions in the picture and circle the differences.

Example			
Student A	A man's jogging on the path.	**Student B**	Two women are sitting on a bench.
Student B	Yes, I see him.	**Student A**	Sorry, I don't see them.

> **Memo**
> Don't look at Student B's picture.

Vocabulary						
ACTIONS			**THINGS**			
• catch	• feed	• hold	• baseball	• bicycle	• ducks
• kick	• ride	• stand	• Frisbee	• path	• soccer
• draw	• fish	• jog	• bench	• football	• entrance
• kneel	• sit	• throw	• grass	• pond	• MP3 player

Speaking task two   Do this exercise in a group of three or more students.

The first student must choose a picture and say what he or she is doing. The next student must repeat the sentence and make one more sentence using a different picture. Each student must repeat every sentence and make one more sentence.

Continue around the circle and use as many pictures as possible, repeating all the sentences (with names) for about fifteen minutes (until your teacher says "stop").

The group of students that uses the most pictures, and correctly repeats the most sentences, wins!

Example

 Harry   I'm doing laundry.

  Alan   Harry's doing laundry. I'm reading the newspaper.

   Elaine   Harry's doing laundry. Alan's reading the newspaper. I'm playing piano.

    Harry   I'm doing laundry. Alan's reading the newspaper. Elaine's playing the piano. I'm fishing.

(continue)

Homework

Find a large picture in a magazine of three or more people doing *different* things. Write what each person in the picture is doing. (Write three or more sentences.) Cut out the picture and bring it to class.

Memo
- Write the sentences on a separate sheet of paper.
- Use one large picture that is big enough for the class to see on the board.

Example

- A man is taking a picture.
- A woman is eating ice cream.
- A woman is reading a book.

Homework review   **Work in a group of three or four students.**

The teacher will put everyone's picture on the board and number each picture.

Memo
- Do this exercise in the next lesson if you have time.
- All questions must be about actions, using *-ing*.

Student A
Choose *any* picture on the board. (It does *not* have to be your picture.) Answer questions ("yes" or "no") until someone guesses the picture.

Students B, C and D
Take turns asking Student A yes/no questions about actions in the pictures until you can guess the correct picture.

Example

Student B	Is someone running?		**Student D**	Is a woman reading?
Student A	No.		**Student A**	Yes.
Student C	Is a man singing?		**Student D**	Is it picture number five?
Student A	No.		**Student A**	Yes!

Language focus

What	are	you / they	doing?
	is	he / she	

→

I'm	playing tennis.
He's / She's	watching TV.
We're / They're	doing homework.

Are	you / they	doing laundry?
Is	he / she	watching TV?

→

Yes,	I	am.
	he / she	is.
	we / they	are.

No,	I'm	not.
	he's / she's	
	we're / they're	

27

Review exercises

Exercise 1

The teacher will give you one of the pictures (1–4) below. There is a question for each picture. Write an answer for the question.

1

Piano mover   Could I have your apartment number?

2

Tourist   We love Hawaii, too! Where are you from?

3

Father   What's Amy doing?

4

Son   Dad! Where's my guitar?

Exercise 2

Read your answer to the class. Do *not* read the question. The class will guess your picture.

Listening task

Exercise 1 20–23

Listen to the conversations (1–4) with your *book closed*. Then open your book and write the number of each conversation next to the correct picture.

☐

☐

☐

☐

Exercise 2 20–23

Listen again and write the *keywords* next to each picture.

Speaking task one   Do this exercise in a group of three or more students.

The first student must choose an object and a place, and say where it is. Everyone must draw it in the room. The next student must repeat where that object is and then say where to put one more object. Each student must first repeat where every object is and then say where to draw one more object.

Continue around the circle and talk about as many objects as possible, drawing and repeating where all the objects are for about fifteen minutes (until your teacher says "stop").

The group of students that talks about the most objects, and correctly repeats every location, wins!

Memo
• You can also draw a line from each object to its place instead of a picture.

Example

 Student A   The laptop's on the big desk, in the middle.

 Student B   The laptop's on the big desk, in the middle. The coffee mugs are on the table, on the right.

Student C   The laptop's on the big desk, in the middle. The coffee mugs are on the table, on the right. The trash can's under the small desk, on the left.

 **Student A**   The laptop's on the big desk, in the middle. The coffee mugs are on the table, on the right. The trash can's under the small desk, on the left. The copier's between the water cooler and the small desk.

(continue)

Vocabulary

• big desk	• shelf	• copier	• printer	• laptop	• CDs
• small desk	• refrigerator	• file folders	• photographs	• plant	• water cooler
• table	• file cabinet	• coffee mugs	• desktop computer	• paper clips	• desk lamp

Speaking task two   Do these exercises in a group of three or more students.

Exercise 1

Student A

Choose any *five* boxes on this page. Act out the action in each box until someone guesses the action correctly.

Students B and C

Close your book and watch Student A. Take turns and guess what Student A is doing. To guess, ask, "Are you ... -ing?"

Example

Student A	[playing piano]
Student B	Are you typing?
Student A	No, I'm not typing.
Student C	Are you playing piano?
Student A	Yes! I'm playing piano.

talking on the phone

drinking coffee

fishing

riding a bicycle

writing a letter

dancing

watching TV

riding a motorcycle

reading the newspaper

listening to music

brushing your teeth

playing chess

driving a car

taking pictures

eating dinner

doing homework

taking a nap

playing piano

getting a haircut

taking a bath

playing soccer

taking a shower

playing tennis

cooking

typing

Exercise 2

Do the exercise again. Act out actions that are *not* on this page. Take turns after each action.

Caller, turn to page 93

Language game   Play this game with two to four "players" and one "caller."

Take turns choosing two numbers (1–24) from the grid below. Each number is a question or an answer. The caller will read each sentence that you choose.

Choose one number, listen to the caller read the sentence and then choose another number. Try to match a question with the answer. Do not write any notes. Just listen!

Continue until all the questions and answers have been matched. The player with the most matches wins!

> **M e m o**
> - Cross off (✗) all matched numbers and circle your matches.
> - Look at this page only!
> - The teacher may let you write notes on the numbers.

Example

Player A	Number 4.	Player B	Number 23.
Caller	"What's she doing?"	Caller	"She's exercising."
Player A	Number 11.	Player B	Number 4.
Caller	"I'm from Italy." They don't match!	Caller	"What's she doing?" They match!

1   2   3   4   5   6

7   8   9   10   11   12

13   14   15   16   17   18

19   20   21   22   23   24

Warm-up exercises

Exercise 1

Write the woman's question.

Exercise 2 24

Listen to the following conversation. Then practice it with a partner.

> **Memo**
>
> Always look at the person you are speaking to. Don't look down at the page!

Jenny	So, what do you do, Pablo?
Pablo	I'm a taxi driver.
Jenny	Oh, really? Do you like it?
Pablo	Yes, I do, but driving in the city isn't easy.
Jenny	How do you get to work?
Pablo	I usually take the subway.

Exercise 3

Practice the conversation again. This time, Pablo cannot look at the page. Answer the questions with *true* information or make up the answers.

Look at page 38

Language focus

Listening task

Exercise 1 25

Listen to each sentence (1–8). Write the number of each sentence on the correct picture below.

Vocabulary

• doctor	• drives	• in a restaurant	• by taxi	• at night	• uniform

Exercise 2 25

Listen to each sentence (1–8) again and write the verb of each sentence below the picture.

Exercise 3 26

Listen to each sentence (1–10) and write the number of the sentence below *any* picture (occupation) on page 35 that it matches.

Memo

Each sentence matches more than one picture.

Example

1　He always works indoors.

Vocabulary

• all night	• always	• customers	• indoors	• sometimes
• office	• alone	• usually	• carries	• on the street

Exercise 4 27–30

Listen to four of the people talk about their jobs. Write the number of each person (1–4) next to the correct picture below.

Vocabulary

OCCUPATIONS

- bellhop
- letter carrier
- traffic cop
- dentist
- taxi driver
- writer

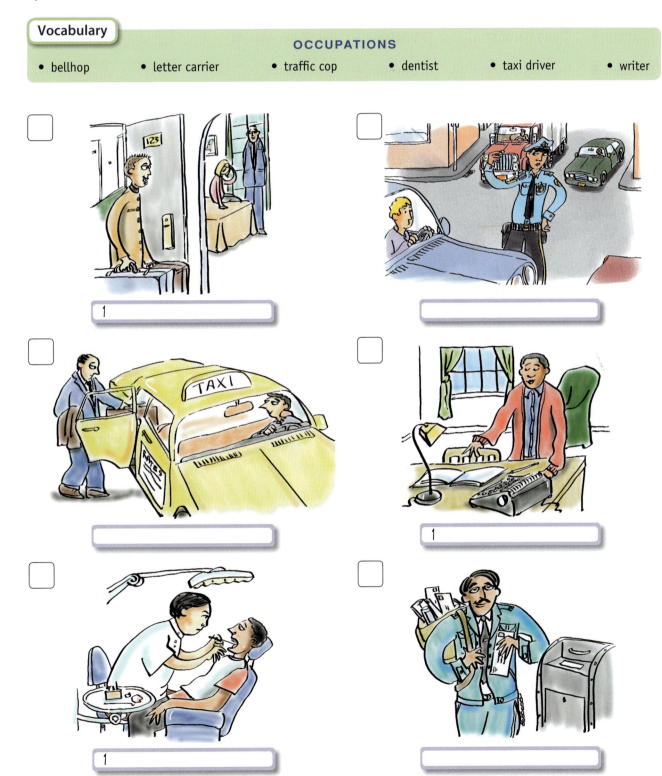

1

1

1

Student B, turn to page 94

Speaking task one   Do Exercise 1 with a partner and Exercise 2 with everyone.

Exercise 1

Ask Student B yes/no questions to find out a person's occupation.

Example			
Student A	Does he wear a uniform?	**Student A**	Does he work at night?
Student B	Yes, he does.	**Student B**	Sometimes.

> **Memo**
> Change roles as Student A and Student B, and do the exercise again.

waiter

cashier

airline pilot

construction worker

hairdresser

janitor

chef

police officer

Vocabulary

- work outdoors
- work at night
- work alone
- sit down at work
- take money from customers
- wear a uniform
- wear a hat
- work indoors

Exercise 2

The teacher will give you one of the occupations above to answer questions about. Walk around and talk to your classmates. Answer questions about your occupation and ask your classmates the above yes/no questions about their occupations. Ask, "Are you (a waiter)?" *after* you have asked all the other questions and write all your classmates' names below their occupations.

Example			
Student A	Do you wear a uniform?	**Student A**	Do you work at night?
Student B	Yes, I do.	**Student B**	Sometimes.

> **Memo**
> Ask only the questions above. Don't ask, "What do you do?"

Student B, turn to page 95

Speaking task two

Take turns with Student B asking and answering questions. Ask Student B for information to fill in the blanks in the chart.

> **Memo**
> Answer in full sentences, but only write *notes* in your blanks.

Name?	Occupation?	Like it?	Where?	How?	Days?
Anna	travel agent	☺	at a travel agency	by taxi	M (Tu) W (Th) F (Sa) (Su)
		○			M Tu W Th F Sa Su
Tony	office manager	☹	in an office building	by car	(M)(Tu)(W)(Th) (F) Sa Su
		○			M Tu W Th F Sa Su
		○ ○			M Tu W Th F Sa Su
Chris and Maria	salesclerks	☹ ☹	in a department store	by subway	M Tu (W)(Th) (F) (Sa) (Su)
Student B		○			M Tu W Th F Sa Su

> **Example**
>
> | | |
> |---|---|
> | Student B | What's her name? |
> | Student A | Her name's Anna. |
> | Student B | What does she do? |
> | Student A | She's a travel agent. |
> | Student B | Does she like it? |
> | Student A | Yes, she does. |
> | Student B | Where does she work? |
> | Student A | She works at a travel agency. |
>
> | | |
> |---|---|
> | Student B | How does she get to work? |
> | Student A | She gets to work by taxi. |
> | Student B | What days does she work? |
> | Student A | She works Tuesday, Thursday, Friday, Saturday and Sunday. |

> **Memo**
> Look at the example for *help* sometimes. Do *not* read the sentences every time you ask or answer.

Homework

Choose any occupation and write six to ten sentences about a person who has the occupation.

Example

(uniform)   He always wears a uniform.

(outdoors)   He does not work outdoors.

Vocabulary

IDEAS

- uniform
- sits down
- hat
- alone
- customers
- at night
- indoors
- outdoors
- in an office
- carries things
- in a restaurant
- in a bank

Homework review   **Work in a group of three or four students.**

The teacher will write everyone's occupation on the board and number each one.

Student A

Choose *any* occupation on the board. Answer questions ("yes" or "no") until someone guesses the occupation.

Students B, C and D

Take turns asking Student A yes/no questions about the occupations until you can guess the correct one.

Example

Student B	Does he wear a uniform?
Student A	Yes, he does.
Student C	Does he wear a hat?
Student A	Yes, he does.

Student D	Does he work outdoors?
Student A	No, he doesn't.
Student D	Is he a bus driver?
Student A	Yes, he is!

Language focus

What	do	you / they	do?		I'm / He's / She's	a teacher.
	does	he / she			We're / They're	teachers.

Do	you / they	sit down at work? work at night?		Yes,	I / we / they	usually	do.
					he / she	sometimes	does.
Does	he / she			No,	I / we / they	don't.	
					he / she	doesn't.	

How	do	you / they	get to work?		I / We / They	get	to work	by bus.
	does	he / she			He / She	gets		by subway.

I / We / They	always usually	work at night.		I / We / They	don't	work outdoors. wear a uniform.
He / She	sometimes	wears a hat.		He / She	doesn't	sit down at work.

7 IN MY FREE TIME
Free time activities

Warm-up exercises

Exercise 1

Write the lighthouse keeper's answer.

So, what do you like to do in your free time?

Exercise 2   🔘 31

Listen to the following conversation. Then practice it with a partner.

Memo

Always look at the person you are speaking to. Don't look down at the page!

Jenny	What do you like to do in your free time, George?
George	I like to go skydiving.
Jenny	Wow! Where do you do that?
George	I go to Sky Ranch, out by the airport.
Jenny	Really? How often do you go?
George	Well, about once a year, maybe. Actually, I did it once.

Exercise 3

Practice the conversation again. This time, George cannot look at the page. Answer the questions with *true* information or make up the answers.

Look at page 43 · Language focus

Listening task

Exercise 1 32–34

Listen to the conversations (1–3). Write the number of each conversation on the activities that are mentioned.

Exercise 2 32–34

Listen to the conversations again. Below each activity, make a note of **(1)** *where* they do it, **(2)** *how often* they do it, **(3)** *when* they do it or **(4)** *who* they do it with.

Vocabulary

- paint
- read magazines
- take pictures

- go dancing
- go jogging
- go shopping

- go bowling
- go to the library
- go to the movies

- play golf
- play ping-pong

Speaking task one   Do Exercise 1 alone and Exercise 2 with everyone.

Exercise 1

Memo
- In Exercise 2, ask and answer in full sentences.
- Write the correct verb form (-s).

Circle one answer on each line (1–5). (The answers do *not* have to be true.)
Use these as *your* answers in Exercise 2.

1	**What?**	• play basketball	• listen to music	• go swimming	• read
2	**Where?**	• at home	• at school	• in the park	• at a friend's house
3	**How often?**	• every day	• once a week	• twice a month	• once a month
4	**When?**	• in the morning	• in the afternoon	• in the evening	• on the weekend
5	**Who / with?**	• with my friend	• with my brother	• with my sister	• alone

Exercise 2

Walk around the classroom and ask your classmates the questions in Exercise 1. Write one classmate's name and activity in each box below. When you have four *different* names in a line, shout "Bingo!" and sit down.

Example

Student A	What do you like to do in your free time?
Student B	I like to read.
Student A	Where do you read?
Student B	I read at home.

John
name
reads
activity
at home

name	name	name	name
activity	activity	activity	activity
once a week	at home	in the morning	with a friend

name	name	name	name
activity	activity	activity	activity
with his/her sister	in the afternoon	in the park	every day

name	name	name	name
activity	activity	activity	activity
at school	twice a month	with his/her brother	in the evening

name	name	name	name
activity	activity	activity	activity
on the weekend	alone	once a month	at a friend's house

Example

- Where do you play basketball?
- How often do you play basketball?
- When do you play basketball?
- Who do you play basketball with?

Speaking task two   Do Exercise 1 alone and Exercise 2 with everyone.

Exercise 1

Look at the pictures below. Circle four activities that you like to do.

Vocabulary

- play pool
- go hiking
- play cards
- go fishing
- play volleyball
- go horseback riding

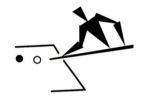

Exercise 2

Walk around the classroom and ask about the twelve activities that you did *not* circle. For each activity, find one person who likes to do it and write his/her name, and **(1)** *where* he/she does it, **(2)** *how often* he/she does it, **(3)** *when* he/she does it and **(4)** *who* he/she does it with.

Memo

- Answer in complete sentences.
- Don't let anyone see your book.

Example

Student A	Do you like to go fishing?		**Student A**	Where do you go fishing?
Student B	Yes, I do.		**Student B**	I usually go to Lake Placid.

Homework

Choose any three activities that you like to do in your free time. For each one, write **(1)** *where* you do it, **(2)** *how often* you do it, **(3)** *when* you do it and **(4)** *who* you do it with.

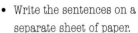
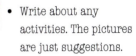

Homework review   Work in a group of three or four students.

The teacher will write everyone's activities on the board.

Student A

Do *not* tell the group which activities you wrote about. Answer questions until someone guesses each activity.

Students B, C and D

Take turns asking Student A questions about each activity. Ask questions about *where*, *how often*, *when* and *who / with*, and try to guess each activity.

Example

Student B	Where do you do it?
Student A	I do it at school.
Student C	How often do you do it?
Student A	I do it about twice a month.

Student D	Who do you usually do it with?
Student A	I do it with my friends.
Student B	You play basketball!
Student A	That's right!

Language focus

| What | do | you / they | like to do in | your / their | free time? | → | I / We / They | like | | to | play tennis. |
| | does | he / she | like to do in | his / her | | | He / She | likes | | | go jogging. |

| How often / Where | do | you / they | play tennis? | → | I / We / They | play tennis / go jogging | every day. every Saturday. |
| | does | he / she | go jogging? | | He / She | plays tennis / goes jogging | in the park. at school. |

| Who | do | you | play tennis / go jogging | with? | → | I | play tennis / go jogging | with friends. |
| | does | he / she | | | | He / She | plays tennis / goes jogging | alone. |

Warm-up exercises

Exercise 1

Write the customer's question.

Exercise 2   35

Listen to the following conversation. Then practice it with a partner.

Denise	Do you have the first aid kit?
John	Yeah, it's in my backpack.
Denise	How much cash do we have?
John	Let's see, I have about $250.
Denise	I have $175. Oh, I don't have the car keys. Do you?
John	Yeah, I have them. OK, let's go.

> **Memo**
>
> Always look at the person you are speaking to. Don't look down at the page!

Exercise 3

Practice the conversation again. This time, John cannot look at the page. Answer the questions with the same information or make up the answers.

Look at page 48
Language focu

44

Listening task

Exercise 1 36

Listen and circle all the items below that are mentioned in the conversation.

> **Vocabulary**
>
> - camping stove
> - compass
> - flashlight
> - tent
> - umbrellas
> - insect spray
> - forks and knives
> - canteen
> - cell phone
> - guidebooks
> - pots and pans
> - camera
> - sleeping bags
> - alarm clock
> - mugs and plates
> - maps

Exercise 2 36

Listen again and write "D" on the things that Denise has and "J" on the things that John has.

Speaking task one

Exercise 1

These pictures of movie stars and their possessions are different from Student B's pictures. Ask and answer questions about their possessions and circle the items that are different.

M e m o
Don't look at Student B's pictures.

Example

Student A Does Denzel have a helicopter?	**Student B** Does he have a motorcycle?
Student B No, he doesn't.	**Student A** Yes, he does.

Vocabulary

- tennis court
- helicopter
- sailboat
- motorcycle
- speedboat
- airplane
- parrot
- bicycle
- swimming pool

Julia

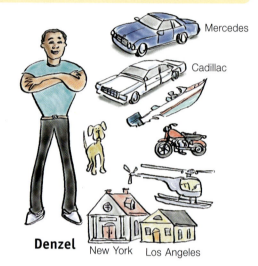

Denzel

Mel

Bill and Sharon

Exercise 2

Talk about things you and Student B have and do *not* have. Make three lists of as many things as you can on a piece of paper: **(1)** things you have, but Student B does *not*, **(2)** things Student B has, but you do *not* and **(3)** things you *both* have.

Example

Student A I have a guitar. Do you?	
Student B No, I don't.	
Student B I have a cat. Do you?	
Student A Yes, I have a cat, too.	

Speaking task two Do this exercise with everyone.

The teacher will give you one of the boxes (1–6) below. Walk around the classroom and ask yes/no questions. If the answer is "yes," write down the name of the person. Then ask, "What kind do you have?" and write down the answer.

Memo

- Change partners after you ask and answer questions about one object.
- Give true answers.

Vocabulary

- snowboard
- pair of skis
- camcorder
- electronic dictionary
- pet
- DVD player
- pair of sneakers
- musical instrument
- tennis racket

Example

Student A	Do you have an MP3 player?	Student A	What kind do you have?
Student B	Yes, I do.	Student B	It's a Sony.

1 Find someone who:

_____ (name) has an MP3 player. _____ (kind)

_____ (name) has a camera. _____ (kind)

_____ (name) has a cell phone. _____ (kind)

2 Find someone who:

_____ (name) has a bicycle. _____ (kind)

_____ (name) has a pair of skis. _____ (kind)

_____ (name) has a desktop computer. _____ (kind)

3 Find someone who:

_____ (name) has a snowboard. _____ (kind)

_____ (name) has a DVD player. _____ (kind)

_____ (name) has a musical instrument. _____ (kind)

4 Find someone who:

_____ (name) has a pet. _____ (kind)

_____ (name) has a camera phone. _____ (kind)

_____ (name) has a laptop computer. _____ (kind)

5 Find someone who:

_____ (name) has a watch. _____ (kind)

_____ (name) has a calculator. _____ (kind)

_____ (name) has a pair of sneakers. _____ (kind)

6 Find someone who:

_____ (name) has a pair of jeans. _____ (kind)

_____ (name) has a tennis racket. _____ (kind)

_____ (name) has a camcorder. _____ (kind)

Homework

Make *two* lists of things. List six things that you or other members of your family have and six things that you or other members of your family do *not* have but would *like* to have.

Then write a sentence about each of the twelve things on your lists.

Example

- I have a laptop computer.
- My sister doesn't have a snowboard.

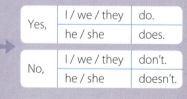

Homework review **Do this exercise with everyone.**

Walk around the classroom and talk to your classmates. Ask about the twelve things on your lists. For each thing, find someone who has one or whose family member has one, and write that person's name next to your sentence.

Example

Student A	Does anyone in your family have a laptop computer?
Student B	Yes, my sister does.

Student B	Does anyone in your family have a snowboard?
Student C	No, no one does.

Language focus

Do	you / they	have	a CD player? headphones?
Does	he / she		

Yes,	I / we / they	do.
	he / she	does.

No,	I / we / they	don't.
	he / she	doesn't.

What kind of	MP3 player	do	you / they	have?
	headphones	does	he / she	

It's a	Sony.
They're	Panasonic.

I / You / We / They	have	a motorcycle.
He / She	has	two dogs.

I / You / We / They	don't	have	a cat.
He / She	doesn't		sunglasses.

9 I'LL TAKE TWO
Buying things

Warm-up exercises

Exercice 1

Write the man's question.

?

This one is $15,000.

Exercise 2  37

Listen to the following conversation. Then practice it with a partner.

Memo

Always look at the person you are speaking to. Don't look down at the page!

Salesclerk	Can I help you?
Alexander	I'm looking for a birthday present for my girlfriend. How much is that necklace?
Salesclerk	This one? It's $299.
Alexander	Oh. Well, how much are those earrings over there?
Salesclerk	Those small ones? They're $49 a pair.
Alexander	OK, I'll take one earring.

Exercise 3

Practice the conversation again. This time, the salesclerk cannot look at the page. Answer the questions with the same information or make up the answers.

Look at page 53

Language focus

Listening task

Exercise 1   38–40

What are the people buying? Listen to each conversation (1–3) and circle all the things that each shopper buys.

Exercise 2   38–40

Listen to each conversation again. Write how many of each thing the shopper buys. Then add up how much money each shopper spends.

Vocabulary

- toothbrush
- baby powder
- aspirin
- nail clippers
- Band-Aids

Vocabulary

- fruitcake
- cookies
- doughnuts
- French bread
- pie

Vocabulary

- memory card
- battery
- lens cap
- photo album

Salesperson, turn to page 97

Speaking task one   Do Exercise 1 alone and Exercise 2 with different partners.

Exercise 1

Circle eight items below to buy from the hardware store.

About ⅔ of the class will be shoppers and about ⅓ of the class will be salespeople (at different stores).

- tape measure
- broom
- paintbrush
- hammer
- light bulbs
- work gloves
- trash can
- nails
- rope
- thumbtacks
- extension cord
- trash bags

Exercise 2

You are a shopper with only $30. Talk to a salesperson and buy the things you need. Check (✓) each item you buy and write the price. If the salesperson does *not* have an item or if it is too *expensive*, talk to a salesperson at a different hardware store.

- The shoppers walk around to buy things.
- The salespeople stay in their seats.
- Change roles as shoppers and salespeople, and do the exercises again.

Example

Shopper	Excuse me, I'm looking for a hammer.
Salesperson	Sure, we have hammers.
Shopper	How much are they?
Salesperson	They're $3.95 each.
Shopper	OK, I'll take one.
Salesperson	Can I help you?
Shopper	Do you have trash cans?
Salesperson	No, we don't. Sorry.
Shopper	Thanks, anyway.

51

Speaking task two

The picture of the shops below is different from Student B's picture. Ask and answer questions about the items and prices in the picture. Circle any item or price that is *different*.

<table>
<tr><td colspan="2">**Example**</td></tr>
<tr><td>Student A</td><td>Do they have carrots in the fruit and vegetables shop?</td></tr>
<tr><td>Student B</td><td>Yes, they do.</td></tr>
<tr><td>Student A</td><td>How much are they?</td></tr>
<tr><td>Student B</td><td>They're 49 cents a pound.</td></tr>
<tr><td>Student A</td><td>That's the same.</td></tr>
<tr><td></td><td></td></tr>
<tr><td>Student B</td><td>Do they have rabbits in the pet shop?</td></tr>
<tr><td>Student A</td><td>Yes, they do.</td></tr>
<tr><td>Student B</td><td>How much are they?</td></tr>
<tr><td>Student A</td><td>They're $9.50.</td></tr>
<tr><td>Student B</td><td>That's different. They're $19.50.</td></tr>
</table>

Memo

- Don't look at Student B's picture.
- Always use the plural form (*peppers, caps, lamps, rabbits*, etc.).

Vocabulary

- carrots
- peppers
- onions
- bananas
- grapes
- strawberries

Vocabulary

- belts
- boots
- caps
- sweaters
- T-shirts
- jackets

Vocabulary

- coffee makers
- hair dryers
- lamps
- CD players
- tea kettles
- toasters

Vocabulary

- turtles
- fish
- monkeys
- parrots
- rabbits
- snakes

Homework

Write the lines of this dialogue *in order* and begin each line with "Customer" or "Salesperson." ("Salesperson" lines are in blue boxes.) Line numbers 3 and 9 have been marked.

Memo

Write the dialogue on a separate sheet of paper.

Oh, OK. Thank you very much.

It's six dollars for 500 sheets.

Sure, they're on the left, right over there.

Well, I only need four. Also, do you have copier paper?

How much is it?

No, we don't. They're on the second floor, in the toy department.

3 I see. How much are they?

Excuse me, I'm looking for plastic report covers.

9 OK, thanks. Oh, do you have crayons?

Yes, it's in the next aisle.

They're two for a dollar or $4.95 a dozen.

Sure. Have a nice day.

Homework review   Do this exercise with a partner.

Practice the dialogue with a partner and make sure all your lines are in the correct order.

Memo

• Do this exercise in the next lesson if you have time.
• Always look at your partner when you are speaking.

Language focus

| How much | is | this / that | shirt? | → | It's | twenty-five dollars and fifty cents. |
| | are | these / those | shoes? | | They're | forty-seven fifty. |

| Do you have | raincoats? / toy trains? | → | Yes, we do. / No, I'm sorry, we don't. | I'll take / Let me have | one. / two. |

10 SAY THAT AGAIN

Review and consolidation

Review exercises

Memo

- Write on a separate sheet of paper.
- If you finish early, write an answer for *another* picture.

Exercise 1

The teacher will give you one of the pictures (1–4) below. There is a question for each picture. Write an answer for the question.

1

Boy   Excuse me, how much is the movie?

2

Woman   Do you have any pets?

3

Woman   So, young man, what do you do?

4

Woman   How often do you eat carrots, Norbert?

Exercise 2

Read your answer to the class. Do *not* read the question. The class will guess your picture.

Memo

Try to memorize your answer for Exercise 2.

Listening task

Exercise 1 41–44

Listen to the conversations (1–4) with your *book closed*. Then open your book and write the number of each conversation next to the correct picture.

Exercise 2 41–44

Listen again and write the *keywords* next to each picture.

Player, turn to page 99

Caller

Speaking task one   Play this game with one "caller" and two to four "players."

Choose any picture below and make up a statement or question. Tell the players the sentence. Continue to choose pictures and tell the players sentences until one player shouts "Bingo!"

Example

 Caller   She works in a hospital.

 Caller   Do they have a house?

 Caller   She listens to music and plays tennis in her free time.

(continue)

Memo
- Use each picture only one time.
- You can use two or three pictures in one sentence if you like.
- Say each sentence two times.

Speaking task two
Do these exercises in a group of three or more students.

Exercise 1

Student A
Choose any *five* boxes on this page. Act out the action in each box until someone guesses the action correctly.

Students B and C
Close your book and watch Student A. Take turns and guess what Student A does every day. To guess, ask, "Do you … every day?"

Example

Student A	[play piano]
Student B	Do you use your computer every day?
Student A	No, I don't use my computer every day.
Student C	Do you play piano every day?
Student A	Yes! I play piano every day.

cook

do laundry

write letters

talk on the phone

go swimming

watch TV

play piano

take a nap

ride your bicycle

ride a motorcycle

take pictures

use your computer

read the newspaper

take a bath

listen to music

exercise

type

drink coffee

go shopping

play tennis

take a shower

play chess

take a bus

brush your teeth

do homework

Exercise 2

Do the exercise again. Act out actions that are *not* on this page. Take turns after each action.

Caller, turn to page 100

Language game   Play this game with two to four "players" and one "caller."

Take turns choosing two numbers (1–24) from the grid below. Each number is a question or an answer. The caller will read each sentence that you choose.

Choose one number, listen to the caller read the sentence and then choose another number. Try to match a question with the answer. Do not write any notes. Just listen!

Continue until all the questions and answers have been matched. The player with the most matches wins!

M e m o

- Cross off (✗) all matched numbers and circle your matches.
- Look at this page only!
- The teacher may let you write notes on the numbers.

Example

Player A	Number 4.	**Player B**	Number 23.
Caller	"What does he do?"	**Caller**	"He's a bus driver."
Player A	Number 11.	**Player B**	Number 4.
Caller	"It's a Nikon." They don't match!	**Caller**	"What does he do?" They match!

1   2   3   4   5   6

7   8   9   10   11   12

13   14   15   16   17   18

19   20   21   22   23   24

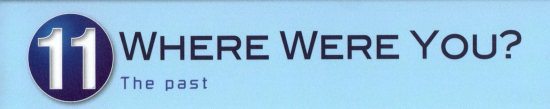
Warm-up exercises

Exercise 1

Write the man's answer.

Exercise 2 ⊙ 45

Listen to the following conversation. Then practice it with a partner.

> **Memo**
>
> Always look at the person you are speaking to. Don't look down at the page!

Alan	Hey, Betsy! Where were you yesterday?
Betsy	Hi, Alan. I was at home. Why?
Alan	I called you three times.
Betsy	Ah, I was out in the garden.
Alan	Well, my barbecue was yesterday.
Betsy	Oh, no, the barbecue! I forgot! Sorry.

Exercise 3

Practice the conversation again. This time, Betsy cannot look at the page. Answer the questions with the same information or make up the answers.

Look at page 64

Language focus

Listening task

Exercise 1 46–51

Where were these people yesterday? Listen to the conversations and number the places from one to six.

1
Jenny

2
Bruce

3
Colin and Lisa

4
Ed

5
Fern

6
Gina and Tom

Vocabulary

- the airport
- the hairdresser
- the beach
- the dentist's office
- the mall
- the park
- an auto shop
- a restaurant
- home
- flight
- haircut
- pick up
- stay in bed
- sick
- terrible

 *North Mall*

 *Diner*

Exercise 2 46–51

Listen again and make a short note of what each person did at each place.

Example

 North Mall

went shopping

Student B, turn to page 101

Speaking task one

Exercise 1 — Work alone.

Memo
In Exercise 1 and Exercise 2, keep the "couples" together!

You decide where these people (1–4) were yesterday. Write the name(s) in a blank next to four different places.

Vocabulary
- the mall
- the park
- school
- the library
- home
- work

ANSWER

1 Amy   2 Bill   3 Cheri and Dan   4 (your name)

Exercise 2 — Work with a partner.

Memo
- In Exercise 2, don't ask *where* questions.
- Try to finish first!

Take turns with Student B asking and answering questions (*one* question each turn):

- Answer Student B's questions about the people (1–4) above.
- Ask Student B *only* yes/no questions about the people (5–8) below and write the names in the blanks next to the places.

ASK

5 Eve   6 Fred   7 Harry and Gina   8 (Student B)

Example

| Student A | Was Eve at the park yesterday? |
| Student B | No, she wasn't. |

| Student B | Were Cheri and Dan at home yesterday? |
| Student A | Yes, they were. |

Exercise 3 — Work with everyone.

Memo
- In Exercise 3, don't ask yes/no questions.
- Try to finish first!

Walk around the classroom and ask different classmates *where* they were yesterday. Write each classmate's name next to the place. Continue until every blank has a name.

Example

| Student A | Where were you yesterday? |
| Student C | I was at the park. |

name(s)
name(s)
name(s)
name(s)
name(s)
name(s)
name(s)
name(s)
name(s)
name(s)

11

Speaking task two

Exercise 1 — Work alone.

You were on vacation last week.

- Choose *five* places (on page 63) and write the day you were at each place: M., Tu., W., Th., F.
- Write *one* activity you did at each place on the line below it. (Choose a *different* activity for each place from the vocabulary box below.)

> **Memo**
> Don't write "I went to ... ."

Example

M.

I played tennis.

Vocabulary

ACTIVITIES

- buy stamps
- buy cat food
- work out
- do homework
- go jogging
- go swimming
- have lunch
- walk around
- listen to music
- watch TV

- look at computers
- look at clothes
- mail a package
- look at things
- play tennis
- play cards
- read a book
- read the newspaper
- study for a test
- study English

- (You can also choose your *own* activity.)

Exercise 2 — Work with a partner.

Find out where your partner was on Monday through Friday last week and write the day on each place. Also write what your partner did at each place.

Example

Student A	Where were you last Tuesday?
Student B	I was at the park.
Student A	What did you do there?
Student B	I went jogging.

M.

Tu.

I played tennis.
Mary went jogging.

Exercise 3 — Work with everyone.

Walk around and talk to your classmates. Find someone who went to any place that *you* or *your partner* did *not* go to. Write the day and a sentence for each one.

Example

Student A	Were you at the pet store last week?
Student C	Yes, I was, on Friday.
Student A	What did you do there?
Student C	I looked at dogs.

F.

PET STORE

John looked at dogs.

Vocabulary

- the park
- the beach
- the post office
- the library
- the mall
- the gym
- a computer store
- my friend's house
- a pet store
- home

Homework

Write seven sentences about where you were each day last week. Write about a *different* place each day and what you did there. (It does *not* have to be true.)

Example

- On Monday I was at the park. I played basketball.
- On Tuesday I was at a friend's house. I played cards.
- On Wednesday I was ...

Vocabulary

- the park
- the mountains
- the beach
- the bank
- the post office
- the supermarket
- the library
- the gym
- the mall
- a bookstore
- a computer store
- a pet store
- my friend's house
- a party
- school
- home

Homework review Do this exercise with everyone.

Walk around the classroom and talk to your classmates. Ask about each day last week. For each day, find someone who was at the *same place* as you on that day. Ask the person what he or she did there. Make a note of his or her name and the answers (day, place and activity).

Example

Student A	Where were you on Monday?
Student B	I was at the park.
Student A	So was I! What did you do there?
Student B	I played basketball.

Student B	Were you at the mall on Tuesday?
Student C	No, I wasn't.

Language focus

Where	was	he / she	yesterday?		I / He / She	was	(at) home.
	were	you / they	last Monday?		We / They	were	at school.

Was	I / he / she	(at) home? at school? here? there?		Yes,	I / he / she	was.
					you / we / they	were.
Were	you / we / they			No,	I / he / she	wasn't.
					you / we / they	weren't.

What did	you they he she	do	yesterday? at the park?		I He / She We / They	went	to school. to the bank.
						played	basketball. chess.

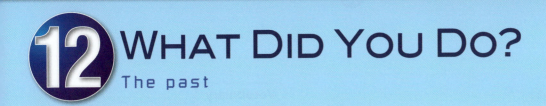

Warm-up exercises

Write the man's answer.

  52

Listen to the following conversation. Then practice it with a partner.

Memo

Always look at the person you are speaking to. Don't look down at the page!

Jane	Did you have a good weekend?
David	Yeah, I went to the beach. What did you do?
Jane	I stayed home.
David	Why did you stay at home?
Jane	I studied for the big test.
David	Test? I didn't hear about a test!

Practice the conversation again. This time, David cannot look at the page. Answer the questions with the same information or make up the answers.

Look at page 69

Language focus

65

Listening task

Exercise 1 53

Darren just came home from shopping at the mall. Listen and number the things you hear.

Exercise 2 53

Listen to the conversation again and check (✓) the things Darren bought.

Speaking task one Do this exercise in a group of three or more students.

The first student must choose a picture and say what he or she did yesterday. The next student must repeat the sentence and make one more sentence using a different picture. Each student must repeat *every* sentence and make one more sentence.

Continue around the circle and use as many pictures as possible, repeating all the sentences (with names) for about fifteen minutes (until your teacher says "stop").

The group of students that uses the most pictures, and correctly repeats the most sentences, wins!

Example

 Harry   I read a magazine.

  Alan   Harry read a magazine. I went to the airport.

   Elaine   Harry read a magazine. Alan went to the airport. I went to the doctor.

    Harry   I read a magazine. Alan went to the airport. Elaine went to the doctor. I visited a friend.

(continue)

12

Student B, turn to page 102

Student A

Speaking task two

Exercise 1

Take turns with Student B asking and answering questions about what the people below did last weekend. For the empty boxes, find out the following information and write it in one or two sentences: **(1)** *what* they did, **(2)** *when* they did it, **(3)** *where* they did it, **(4)** *who* they did it with and **(5)** *how long* they did it.

Memo

Answer each question separately. Don't read the sentence to Student B.

Example

Student B What did Naoko do last weekend?
Student A She played tennis.

Student B Where did she play?
Student A She played at the park.

Naoko played tennis at the park with her younger sister for about three hours on Sunday morning.

Naoko

Paul

Antonio

Monica went shopping at the mall for about six hours on Saturday afternoon with her friends.

Monica

Lina and Marco went hiking on Sunday in the mountains with their classmates. They went hiking all day, for about eight hours.

Lina and Marco

Luke and Sara

Exercise 2

Ask Student B similar questions about what he or she did last weekend. Write all the information in one or two sentences.

Memo

Take turns asking and answering questions.

Student B

Homework

Find a large picture in a magazine of three or more people doing different things. Write a sentence about each person in the *past tense*. Cut out the picture and bring it to class.

Memo

- Write the sentences on a separate sheet of paper.
- Use one large picture that is big enough for the class to see on the board.

Example

- A woman went shopping.
- A man rode a motorcycle.
- A woman took a bus.

Homework review   Work in a group of three or four students.

The teacher will put everyone's picture on the board and number each picture.

Memo

- Do this exercise in the next lesson if you have time.
- All questions must be about actions, using the *past tense*.

Student A

Choose *any* picture on the board. (It does *not* have to be your picture.) Answer questions ("yes" or "no") until someone guesses the picture.

Students B, C and D

Take turns asking Student A yes/no questions about actions in the pictures until you can guess the correct picture.

Example

Student B	Did someone play piano?
Student A	No, no one played piano.
Student C	Did a man sing?
Student A	No, a man didn't sing.

Student D	Did a woman go shopping?
Student A	Yes, a woman went shopping.
Student D	Is it picture number five?
Student A	Yes, it is!

Language focus

| Did | you he / she they | go | to school? jogging? | → | Yes, | I he / she | did. |
| | | play | tennis? piano? | | No, | we / they | didn't. |

| Who | did | you / they he / she | play tennis go jogging | with? | → | I / We / They He / She | played tennis went jogging | with friends. with classmates. |

| Where When | did | you / they he / she | play tennis? go jogging? | → | I / We / They He / She | played tennis went jogging | in the park. on Sunday. |

69

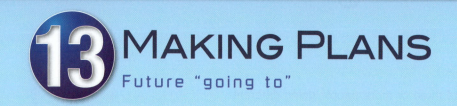

13 MAKING PLANS
Future "going to"

Warm-up exercises

Write the woman's answer.

54

Listen to the following conversation. Then practice it with a partner.

> **Memo**
>
> Always look at the person you are speaking to. Don't look down at the page!

Katie	Are you going to do anything this summer?
Jerry	Yeah, I'm going to fly to Nepal.
Katie	Wow! What are you going to do there?
Jerry	I'm going to go hiking in the Himalayas.
Katie	Really? How long are you going to stay?
Jerry	About a month.

Practice the conversation again. This time, Jerry cannot look at the page. Answer the questions with *true* information or make up the answers.

Look at page 74 Language focus

70

Listening task

Exercise 1 55–57

Listen to three conversations. Circle all the activities that are mentioned in each conversation.

Vocabulary

- go water skiing
- go swimming
- go sailing
- go hiking
- go scuba diving
- go horseback riding
- go to the gym
- go to the sauna
- go to the disco
- play tennis
- play pool
- play volleyball
- see the fireworks
- see the magic show
- see a movie

Exercise 2 55–57

Listen to each conversation again. Write the number of each conversation (1–3) on the activities they are *both* going to do.

Student B, turn to page 103

Speaking task one

Exercise 1   Work alone.

Fill in *any* ten boxes in Chart A using the actions in the pictures below (or on pages 71 or 74). Fill in the other five boxes with a question mark (*?*).

> **Memo**
> - Write notes in the boxes, not sentences.
> - Use each action only one time.

Example

play cards

Chart A	Annie	James	Tim and Kris	Grace	Fran and Larry
Saturday morning					
Saturday afternoon					
Saturday evening					

Exercise 2   Work with a partner.

Look at Chart A above and answer Student B's questions about the people. When you have finished, look at Chart B on page 103. Ask Student B what the people in Chart B are going to do and fill in the boxes.

> **Memo**
> *?* = "I don't know."

Example

Student B	What's Annie going to do Saturday morning?	Student B	What are Tim and Kris going to do Saturday afternoon?
Student A	She's going to play tennis.	Student A	I don't know.

Exercise 3   Work with everyone.

Walk around the classroom, and ask and answer questions. Find answers for all the boxes with a question mark (*?*) in Chart A and Chart B.

Speaking task two   Do Exercise 1 alone and Exercise 2 with everyone.

Exercise 1

Write what you are going to do this weekend. Include as much information as you can for each time of day (the morning, afternoon and evening).

SATURDAY

morning

afternoon

evening

SUNDAY

morning

afternoon

evening

Exercise 2

Walk around the classroom and talk to your classmates about this weekend. For each time of day below (Saturday morning, Saturday afternoon, etc.), talk to a different classmate and write down what he or she is going to do. Ask questions, such as *what*, *who*, *where*, *when* and *how*, and write down as much information as you can.

Example

Student A	What are you going to do Saturday morning?
Student B	I'm going to go to the park.
Student A	Oh, yeah? Who are you going to go with?
Student B	I'm going to go with Sue.

SATURDAY

morning

afternoon

evening

SUNDAY

morning

afternoon

evening

13

Homework

Write about your plans for each day this week (Monday through Sunday).
Choose seven pictures—each one above, under or next to another one—and
write one sentence for each picture.

Memo

• Write on a separate
  sheet of paper.

• Write the day in each of
  your sentences.

Example

• I'm going to go swimming on Monday.
• I'm going to do laundry on Tuesday.

Homework review   Do this exercise with a partner.

Take turns asking and answering yes/no questions, and find out which seven
pictures your partner used. Write the day your partner tells you on each of the
seven pictures. Try to finish before your partner!

Memo

• Do this exercise in the
  next lesson if you have
  time.

• Tell the day when you
  answer.

Example

Student A	Are you going to do laundry this week?	Student B	Are you going to go swimming this week?
Student B	Yes, I'm going to do laundry on Tuesday.	Student A	No, I'm not.

Language focus

Are	you / they	going to	do laundry? go to the library? go swimming?	Yes,	I	am.
					he / she	is.
					we / they	are.
Is	he / she			No,	I'm	not.
					he's / she's	
					we're / they're	

When	are	you / they	going to	play tennis? go shopping?	I'm	going to	play tomorrow.
Where	is	he / she			He's / She's		play at the park.
					We're / They're		go to the mall.

What	are	you / they	going to	do tomorrow? on Sunday?	I'm	going to	play tennis.
	is	he / she			He's / She's		go shopping.
					We're / They're		go to the park.

14 I'LL CALL YOU BACK
On the telephone

Warm-up exercises

Exercise 1

Write the man's answer.

Hello. Can I speak to Jack?

Exercise 2 58

Listen to the following conversation. Then practice it with a partner.

> **Memo**
>
> Always look at the person you are speaking to. Don't look down at the page!

Monica	Hello? May I speak to William, please?
William	Speaking.
Monica	Hi, this is Monica.
William	Oh, hi, Monica. Listen, I'm sorry, but I'm really busy. Can I call you back?
Monica	Oh, sure. I'm at home.
William	OK, bye.
Monica	Bye.

Exercise 3

Practice the conversation again. This time, William cannot look at the page. Answer with the same replies or make up the replies.

Look at page 79

Language focus

75

Listening task

Exercise 1 59–62

Close your book and listen to each conversation (1–4). Open your book and write the number of each conversation next to the correct picture.

Exercise 2 59–62

Listen to the conversations again and write the number (1–4) in the boxes below.

Conversation ☐

A Hello.
B Hello. _____ ?
A Della? I'm sorry, you have the _____.
B Oh, sorry.
A That's OK.

Conversation ☐

A Hello.
B Hello. _____ I speak to Jim, please?
A May I ask _____ ?
B My name is Gina Lombardi. I'm an old friend.
A Sure, hold on just a moment, please.
B OK, thanks.

Conversation ☐

A Hello?
B Hello. _____ I speak to Mike, please?
A _____.
B Mike, it's Dave Zuber. How's everything?
A Hi, Dave! Listen, I can't talk right now. Can I call you back later?
B Sure, no problem. Talk to you later. Bye.
A Bye.

Conversation ☐

A Hello?
B Hello. _____ I speak to Sarah, please?
A Sorry, she's _____.
B Oh, OK. I'll call again later.
A OK, bye.
B Bye.

Exercise 3 59–62

Listen one more time and write the missing words in each conversation.

Student B, turn to page 104

Student A

Speaking task one

Choose *one* of the twelve people below. This is *you*. For each of the other eleven people, check (✓) one of the following:

- "In" (This person lives with you and is at home.)
- "Out" (This person lives with you, but is *not* at home.)
- "Wrong number" (This person does *not* live with you.)

Student B will call to ask for someone. Look at your chart below and answer Student B.

		In	Out	Wrong number				In	Out	Wrong number
1	Anna	☐	☐	☐	7	Gary	☐	☐	☐
2	Barry	☐	☐	☐	8	Helen	☐	☐	☐
3	Charlie	☐	☐	☐	9	Iris	☐	☐	☐
4	Donna	☐	☐	☐	10	Jeff	☐	☐	☐
5	Ed	☐	☐	☐	11	Kris	☐	☐	☐
6	Fran	☐	☐	☐	12	Larry	☐	☐	☐

Example

Student B	May I speak to Fran, please?
Student A	Speaking.
Student B	Could I speak to Helen?
Student A	Sorry, she's out right now.
Student B	Can I speak to Ed?
Student A	Sure, just a moment.
Student B	May I speak to Charlie?
Student A	I'm sorry. You have the wrong number.

See Language focus (page 79) for more examples.

Speaking task two

Memo

Say, "Ring, ring!" to begin each time.

Student A

Fill in the blank below each person in the house with one of the four "notes" below. (Write "Me" on only one of the people.)

Student B will call ("Ring, ring!"). Answer the telephone (look at your notes below) and have a short conversation with Student B.

Notes
- "Me" (This person is you!)
- "In" (This person lives with you and is at home.)
- "Out" (This person lives with you, but is *not* at home.)
- "Wrong number" (This person does *not* live with you.)

Student B

Call Student A's house eight times and ask for one of the people in the house each time. After you speak to Student A, write one of these "notes" in each blank.

Notes
- "Student A" (This person is Student A.)
- "In" (This person lives there and is at home.)
- "Out" (This person lives there, but is *not* at home.)
- "Wrong number" (This person does *not* live there.)

Student A's house

Billy Lisa Rob Diane

Mike Carol Betsy Chuck

Example

Student B	Ring, ring!
Student A	Hello?
Student B	Hello. Is Billy there?
Student A	I'm sorry, he's not in.
Student B	Oh, OK. I'll call again later. Bye.
Student A	Bye-bye.

Billy
out

Memo

Change roles as Student A and Student B, and do the exercise again. (Erase your notes.)

Homework

Write a different reply for each of the blanks below.

Memo

Write the replies on a separate sheet of paper.

A   Hello. Is Alan there?
B

A   Can I speak to Connie, please?
B

A   Hello. Is Elise home?
B

A   Could I speak to Ben?
B

A   May I speak to Debby?
B

A   Could I speak to Frank, please?
B

Homework review   Do this exercise with everyone.

Walk around the classroom and talk to your classmates. Take turns asking the above questions and replying. For each question, find someone who wrote the *same* reply as you and write that person's name below your reply.

Memo

- Do this exercise in the next lesson if you have time.
- If you cannot find anyone, write "no one."

Language focus

	Is Pat there?	
Hello.	Can Could May	I speak to Pat, please?

→

Speaking.
This is Pat.

Sure, just a moment.
Hold on a minute, please.
Yes. May I ask who's calling?

| I'm sorry, | he's she's | not in right now. not here. out right now. |

Sorry, you have the wrong number.

Review exercises

Exercise 1

The teacher will give you one of the pictures (1–4) below. There is a question for each picture. Write an answer for the question.

1

Mother   What did you find in the park?

2

Woman   What are you going to do?

3

Police officer   What's he doing?

4

Doctor   Do you come here often?

Exercise 2

Read your answer to the class. Do *not* read the question. The class will guess your picture.

Listening task

Exercise 1 63–66

Listen to the conversations (1–4) with your *book closed*. Then open your book and write the number of each conversation next to the correct picture.

Memo

You can take notes as you listen.

Exercise 2 63–66

Listen again and write the *keywords* next to each picture.

Memo

Keywords are important words that tell you which picture to choose.

Speaking task one   Do this exercise in a group of three or more students.

Each student must choose a *different* verb tense to use and talk about *now*, *every day*, *yesterday* or *tomorrow*. The first student must choose a picture and say what he or she is *doing*, *usually does*, *did* or is *going to do*. The next student must repeat the sentence and make one more sentence using a different picture. Each student must repeat *every* sentence and make one more sentence.

Continue around the circle and use as many pictures as possible, repeating *all* the sentences (with names) for about fifteen minutes (until your teacher says "stop").

The group of students that uses the most pictures, and correctly repeats the most sentences, wins!

Memo

- Don't write anything on the pictures.
- Help each other repeat the sentences.

Example

 Daisy   I'm doing laundry now.

 George   Daisy's doing laundry now. I read the newspaper every day.

 Susan   Daisy's doing laundry now. George reads the newspaper every day. I saw a movie yesterday.

 Daisy   I'm doing laundry now. George reads the newspaper every day. Susan saw a movie yesterday. I'm going to paint tomorrow.
(continue)

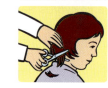

Speaking task two   Do these exercises in a group of three or more students.

Exercise 1

Student A

Choose any *four* actions on this page. For each action, tell the other students which time expression to use (*now*, *every day*, *yesterday* or *tomorrow*). Act out the action until someone guesses the action correctly.

Students B and C

Close your book and watch Student A. Take turns and guess what Student A is doing. Ask yes/no questions only.

Memo

- Review all the actions first.
- Each student take a turn as Student A.
- Use a time expression (*now*, *every day*, *yesterday* or *tomorrow*) in every question.

Example

Student A	I do it every day. [do homework]
Student B	Do you write letters every day?
Student A	No, I don't write letters every day.
Student C	Do you do homework every day?
Student A	Yes! I do homework every day.

Student A	I did it yesterday. [go swimming]
Student B	Did you exercise yesterday?
Student A	No, I didn't exercise yesterday.
Student C	Did you go swimming yesterday?
Student A	Yes! I went swimming yesterday.

ride your bicycle   see a movie   use your computer   do laundry

write letters   take a bath   listen to music

play piano   talk on the phone   play chess

read the newspaper   do homework

take a nap   take pictures   drink coffee

go swimming   ride a motorcycle   take a shower

cook   exercise   take a taxi

go bowling   watch TV

do housework   go jogging

Exercise 2

Do the exercise again. Act out actions that are *not* on this page. Take turns after each action.

Memo

In Exercise 2 you can ask the teacher for help with vocabulary.

Caller, turn to page 105

Language game   Play this game with two to four "players" and one "caller."

Take turns choosing two numbers (1–24) from the grid below. Each number is a question or an answer. The caller will read each sentence that you choose.

Choose one number, listen to the caller read the sentence and then choose another number. Try to match a question with the answer. Do not write any notes. Just listen!

Continue until all the questions and answers have been matched. The player with the most matches wins!

> **Memo**
> * Cross off (✗) all matched numbers and circle your matches.
> * Look at this page only!
> * The teacher may let you write notes on the numbers.

Example

Player A	Number 7.
Caller	"Did you do the homework?"
Player A	Number 12.
Caller	"They went to Italy." They don't match!

Player B	Number 20.
Caller	"No, I didn't. I forgot."
Player B	Number 7.
Caller	"Did you do the homework?" They match!

① ② ③ ④ ⑤ ⑥

⑦ ⑧ ⑨ ⑩ ⑪ ⑫

⑬ ⑭ ⑮ ⑯ ⑰ ⑱

⑲ ⑳ ㉑ ㉒ ㉓ ㉔

APPENDIX

Speaking task one

Exercise 1

Read the sentences about Mary and answer Student A's questions.

Memo

Answer in *short* sentences.

Example

Student A	Is Mary Chinese?
Student B	Yes, she is.
Student A	Does she live near the school?
Student B	No, she doesn't.

Mary is Chinese. She is in this English class. She is not a new student. She does not live near the school. She takes a bus to school.

Exercise 2

Look at each sentence (1–5) and make a yes/no question. Ask Student A each question and check (✓) "Yes" or "No."

Memo

Ask *only* yes/no questions.

Example

Student B	Is Carlos Mexican?
Student A	No, he isn't.
Student B	Does he live near the school?
Student A	Yes, he does.

		Yes	No
1	Carlos is Mexican.	☐	☐
2	He is in this English class.	☐	☐
3	He is a new student.	☐	☐
4	He lives near the school.	☐	☐
5	He takes a bus to school.	☐	☐

Player, turn to page 9

Language game   Play this game with two to four "players" and one "caller."

Before you begin the game, number the questions and answers below from 1 to 16 in *random order* (all mixed up).

The players will take turns choosing two numbers. Listen for the first number and read the first sentence. Listen for the second number, read the second sentence and say if it matches the first sentence or not.* After that, the next player chooses.

Continue until all the questions and answers are matched. The player with the most matches wins!

*You can also ask the players if it is a match before you tell them.

Example			
Player A	Number 4.	**Player B**	Number 16.
Caller	"Could I have your address?"	**Caller**	"Yes, it's 36 Main Street, Dover."
Player A	Number 11.	**Player B**	Number 4.
Caller	"Yes, I do." They don't match!	**Caller**	"Could I have your address?" They match!

Question

Answer

◯ Could you tell me your name, please?	◯ Sure, it's John Moore.
◯ How do you spell "Moore"?	◯ M-O-O-R-E.
◯ Could I have your address?	◯ Yes, it's 36 Main Street, Dover.
◯ Could I have your phone number?	◯ Sure, it's area code 845, 555-2323.
◯ Could I have your student ID number?	◯ Yes, it's 026834.
◯ Could I have your email address?	◯ Yes, it's johnmoore@yippee.com.
◯ Could you tell me your birthday?	◯ Sure, it's March 10th, 1990.
◯ Do you have a passport?	◯ Yes, I do.

Student B

Student A, turn to page 13

Speaking task one

Exercise 1

Look at the information below and answer Student A's questions.

Memo

Answer in *full* sentences.

Example

Student A	Could I have her name?	**Student A**	Where's she from?
Student B	Her name's Eri Park.	**Student B**	She's from Korea.

1

Name: Eri Park

Country: Korea

Languages: Korean and
Japanese

Lives in: Tokyo

2

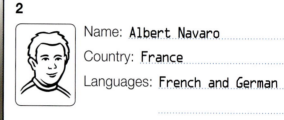

Name: Albert Navaro

Country: France

Languages: French and German

Lives in: Berlin

3

Name: Juan Lopez

Country: Brazil

Languages: Portuguese, Spanish
and English

Lives in: New York

4

Name: Mary Fox

Country: Canada

Languages: French and English

Lives in: London

Exercise 2

Answer Student A's questions about *your* personal information. You can make up the information if you like.

Memo

Change roles as Student A and Student B, and do the exercises again.

Example

Student A	Could I have your name?
Student B	My name's Maria Ramirez.
Student A	Where are you from?
Student B	I'm from Mexico.

Speaking task one

The picture below is different from Student A's picture. Ask and answer questions about the people and things in the picture, and circle anything in a different location.

Memo
- Don't look at Student A's picture.
- You can also ask, "Where is the … ?" or "Where are the … ?"

Example			
Student A	Is the canoe next to the pond?	**Student B**	Are the sleeping bags in the tent?
Student B	Yes, it is.	**Student A**	No, they aren't.

Vocabulary				
• canoe	• pond	• ground	• rock	• cows
• fish	• squirrel	• branch	• grill	• cooler
• tent	• sleeping bags	• firewood	• picnic table	• ax

Speaking task two

Exercise 1

Listen to Student A's questions about the location of the people and objects in the picture below (pages 90 and 91), and tell Student A where each one is.

(pages 90 and 91)

Example

Student A	Where's the letter carrier?
Student B	He's in front of the post office, next to the door, on the right.

Vocabulary

- cat
- letter carrier
- children
- pay phones

- ice cream truck
- taxi cab
- lamp posts
- trash cans

- corner
- playground
- crosswalk
- roof

- lot
- sidewalk
- park
- street

Memo

- Don't look at Student A's book!
- You can also make a simple drawing of the people and objects in the picture.

Student A, turn to pages 20–21

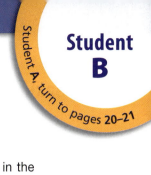

Student B

Exercise 2

Ask Student A for the location of the people and objects below (1–8), and write the numbers in the correct places on the picture (pages 90 and 91).

Example

Student B	Where are the mailboxes?
Student A	They're in front of the post office, next to the door, on the left.

1 mailboxes 2 bicycle 3 bus 4 motorcycle 5 construction workers 6 police officer 7 dogs 8 traffic lights

Speaking task one

The picture of the park scene below is a little different from Student A's picture. Talk about the people's actions in the picture and circle the differences.

Example			
Student A	A man's jogging on the path.	**Student B**	Two women are sitting on a bench.
Student B	Yes, I see him.	**Student A**	Sorry, I don't see them.

Memo

Don't look at Student A's picture.

Vocabulary						
ACTIONS			**THINGS**			
• catch	• feed	• hold	• baseball	• bicycle	• ducks
• kick	• ride	• stand	• Frisbee	• path	• soccer
• draw	• fish	• jog	• bench	• football	• entrance
• kneel	• sit	• throw	• grass	• pond	• MP3 player

Language game   Play this game with two to four "players" and one "caller."

Before you begin the game, number the questions and answers below from 1 to 24 in *random order* (all mixed up).

The players will take turns choosing two numbers. Listen for the first number and read the first sentence. Listen for the second number, read the second sentence and say if it matches the first sentence or not.*
After that, the next player chooses.

Continue until all the questions and answers are matched. The player with the most matches wins!

*You can also ask the players if it is a match before you tell them.

> **Memo**
> - Read each sentence slowly, once or twice.
> - Read both of the sentences before you say, "They match!" or "They don't match!"

Example			
Player A	Number 4.	**Player B**	Number 23.
Caller	"What's she doing?"	**Caller**	"She's exercising."
Player A	Number 11.	**Player B**	Number 4.
Caller	"I'm from Italy." They don't match!	**Caller**	"What's she doing?" They match!

Question	Answer
( ) Could you tell me your name, please?	( ) Sure, it's Linda Lee.
( ) Where are you from?	( ) I'm from Italy.
( ) What's she doing?	( ) She's exercising.
( ) What languages do you speak?	( ) German and Spanish.
( ) Could I have your student ID number?	( ) Yes, it's 166-22-8554.
( ) Where's the teapot?	( ) It's in the kitchen cabinet.
( ) Is Jack sleeping?	( ) No, he's studying English.
( ) Does Anna live in France?	( ) No, she lives in Canada.
( ) What's your address?	( ) It's 169 Main Street.
( ) How do you spell "Italian"?	( ) I-T-A-L-I-A-N.
( ) Where are my slippers?	( ) They're under the bed.
( ) Where are you going?	( ) I'm going home.

Speaking task one

Exercise 1

Choose one occupation. (Do *not* say the occupation.) Answer Student A's questions.

Example

Student A	Does he wear a uniform?	Student A	Does he work at night?
Student B	Yes, he does.	Student B	Sometimes.

Memo

- You can change "he" to "she" and tell Student A the person is a woman.
- Take turns as Student A and Student B.

construction worker
- He does *not* take money from customers.
- He sometimes works outdoors.
- He usually does *not* work at night.
- He does *not* wear a uniform.
- He wears a hat.
- He does *not* sit down at work.
- He does *not* work alone.

police officer
- He sometimes sits down at work.
- He sometimes works at night.
- He wears a hat.
- He usually works outdoors.
- He does *not* take money from customers.
- He usually works alone.
- He wears a uniform.

hairdresser
- He usually works alone.
- He usually does *not* sit down at work.
- He does *not* wear a uniform.
- He takes money from customers.
- He does *not* wear a hat.
- He does *not* work outdoors.
- He usually does *not* work at night.

cashier
- He sometimes works at night.
- He does *not* work outdoors.
- He usually works alone.
- He does *not* wear a hat.
- He does *not* wear a uniform.
- He takes money from customers.
- He usually sits down at work.

janitor
- He does *not* work outdoors.
- He does *not* sit down at work.
- He does *not* take money from customers.
- He usually works alone.
- He does *not* wear a uniform.
- He sometimes works at night.
- He does *not* wear a hat.

waiter
- He does *not* work alone.
- He does *not* work outdoors.
- He usually takes money from customers.
- He wears a uniform.
- He does *not* wear a hat.
- He does *not* sit down at work.
- He sometimes works at night.

chef
- He wears a hat.
- He does *not* work outdoors.
- He does *not* wear a uniform.
- He usually does *not* sit down at work.
- He sometimes works at night.
- He usually does *not* work alone.
- He does *not* take money from customers.

airline pilot
- He sometimes works at night.
- He sits down at work.
- He does *not* take money from customers.
- He does *not* work alone.
- He wears a uniform.
- He usually wears a hat.
- He does *not* work outdoors.

Speaking task two

Take turns with Student A asking and answering questions. Ask Student A for information to fill in the blanks in the chart.

Memo

Answer in full sentences, but only write *notes* in your blanks.

Name?		Occupation?	Like it?	Where?	How?	Days?
			◯			M Tu W Th F Sa Su
Dave		dishwasher	☹	in a hotel restaurant	by bicycle	Ⓜ Tu Ⓦ Th Ⓕ Ⓢⓐ Ⓢⓤ
			◯			M Tu W Th F Sa Su
Nina		librarian	☺	in a college library	by train	M ⓉⓤⓌⓉⓗ Ⓕ Ⓢⓐ Su
Linda and Fred		bakers	☺ ☺	in a bakery	by bus	ⓂⓉⓤⓌⓉⓗ Ⓕ Sa Su
			◯ ◯			M Tu W Th F Sa Su
Student A			◯			M Tu W Th F Sa Su

Example

Student B	What's her name?	**Student B**	How does she get to work?
Student A	Her name's Anna.		
Student B	What does she do?	**Student A**	She gets to work by taxi.
Student A	She's a travel agent.		
Student B	Does she like it?	**Student B**	What days does she work?
Student A	Yes, she does.		
Student B	Where does she work?	**Student A**	She works Tuesday, Thursday, Friday, Saturday and Sunday.
Student A	She works at a travel agency.		

Memo

Look at the example for *help* sometimes. Do *not* read the sentences every time you ask or answer.

Speaking task one

Exercise 1

These pictures of movie stars and their possessions are different from Student A's pictures. Ask and answer questions about their possessions and circle the items that are different.

Memo
Don't look at Student A's pictures.

Example

Student A	Does Denzel have a helicopter?	**Student B**	Does he have a motorcycle?
Student B	No, he doesn't.	**Student A**	Yes, he does.

Vocabulary

- tennis court
- helicopter
- sailboat
- motorcycle
- speedboat
- airplane
- parrot
- bicycle
- swimming pool

Julia

Denzel

Mel

Bill and Sharon

Exercise 2

Talk about things you and Student A have and do *not* have. Make three lists of as many things as you can on a piece of paper: **(1)** things you have, but Student A does *not*, **(2)** things Student A has, but you do *not* and **(3)** things you *both* have.

Example

Student A	I have a guitar. Do you?
Student B	No, I don't.

Student B	I have a cat. Do you?
Student A	Yes, I have a cat, too.

Shopper, turn to page 51

Salesperson

Speaking task one   Do Exercise 1 alone and Exercise 2 with different partners.

Exercise 1

You are a hardware salesperson. Circle *any* six of the items below to sell in your hardware store. (You do *not* have the other six items.) Make up the prices for your six items, between $1.99 and $5.49, and write the price below each item.

Memo

About ⅔ of the class will be shoppers and about ⅓ of the class will be salespeople (at different stores).

Vocabulary

- tape measure
- broom
- paintbrush
- hammer
- light bulbs
- work gloves
- trash can
- nails
- rope
- thumbtacks
- extension cord
- trash bags

Exercise 2

Help the shoppers that come to your hardware store. Count how many items you sell.

Memo

- The shoppers walk around to buy things.
- The salespeople stay in their seats.
- Change roles as shoppers and salespeople, and do the exercises again.

Example

Shopper	Excuse me, I'm looking for a hammer.
Salesperson	Sure, we have hammers.
Shopper	How much are they?
Salesperson	They're $3.95 each.
Shopper	OK, I'll take one.

Salesperson	Can I help you?
Shopper	Do you have trash cans?
Salesperson	No, we don't. Sorry.
Shopper	Thanks, anyway.

Speaking task two

The picture of the shops below is different from Student A's picture. Ask and answer questions about the items and prices in the picture. Circle any item or price that is *different*.

Example

Student A	Do they have carrots in the fruit and vegetables shop?
Student B	Yes, they do.
Student A	How much are they?
Student B	They're 49 cents a pound.
Student A	That's the same.

Student B	Do they have rabbits in the pet shop?
Student A	Yes, they do.
Student B	How much are they?
Student A	They're $9.50.
Student B	That's different. They're $19.50.

Memo

- Don't look at Student A's picture.
- Always use the plural form (*peppers*, *caps*, *lamps*, *rabbits*, etc.).

Vocabulary

- carrots
- peppers
- onions
- bananas
- grapes
- strawberries

Vocabulary

- belts
- boots
- caps
- sweaters
- T-shirts
- jackets

Vocabulary

- coffee makers
- hair dryers
- lamps
- CD players
- tea kettles
- toasters

Vocabulary

- turtles
- fish
- monkeys
- parrots
- rabbits
- snakes

Speaking task one   Play this game with two to four "players" and one "caller."

Choose one of the boxes (1–4) below and use the box to play Bingo. Listen to the caller.
Cross off (✗) any picture that the caller mentions. If you get four "✗s" in a line, shout "Bingo!"

Example

| Caller | She gets to work by bus. |
| Player | [crosses off bus picture] |

> **Memo**
> • Each player choose a different box to start.
> • Play again: each student take a turn as the caller.

1

2

3

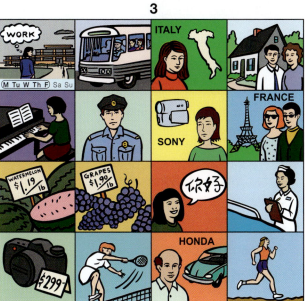

4

Player, turn to page 58

Caller

Language game   Play this game with two to four "players" and one "caller."

Before you begin the game, number the questions and answers below from 1 to 24 in *random order* (all mixed up).

The players will take turns choosing two numbers. Listen for the first number and read the first sentence. Listen for the second number, read the second sentence and say if it matches the first sentence or not.* After that, the next player chooses.

Continue until all the questions and answers are matched. The player with the most matches wins!

*You can also ask the players if it is a match before you tell them.

Memo
- Read each sentence slowly, once or twice.
- Read both of the sentences before you say, "They match!" or "They don't match!"

Example

Player A	Number 4.	**Player B**	Number 23.
Caller	"What does he do?"	**Caller**	"He's a bus driver."
Player A	Number 11.	**Player B**	Number 4.
Caller	"It's a Nikon." They don't match!	**Caller**	"What does he do?" They match!

Question	Answer
◯ What does he do?	◯ He's a bus driver.
◯ Does he wear a uniform at work?	◯ Yes, he does.
◯ How does she get to work?	◯ By bus.
◯ What days does she have off?	◯ She has Sunday and Monday off.
◯ What does she do in her free time?	◯ She goes jogging.
◯ When does she go jogging?	◯ In the evening, around 7:00.
◯ Who do you go to the movies with?	◯ I go with my friends.
◯ Do they have a large house?	◯ No, they don't. It's small.
◯ What kind of camera do they have?	◯ It's a Nikon.
◯ Do you have children's shoes?	◯ No, we don't. Sorry.
◯ How much is this camcorder?	◯ It's $625.
◯ How much are the bananas?	◯ They're 79 cents a pound.

Speaking task one

Student A, turn to page 61

Exercise 1   Work alone.

You decide where these people (1–4) were yesterday. Write the name(s) in a blank next to four different places.

Memo
In Exercise 1 and Exercise 2, keep the "couples" together!

Vocabulary
- the mall
- the park
- school
- the library
- home
- work

ANSWER

1 Eve   2 Fred   3 Harry and Gina   4 (your name)

Exercise 2   Work with a partner.

Memo
- In Exercise 2, don't ask *where* questions.
- Try to finish first!

Take turns with Student A asking and answering questions (*one* question each turn):

- Answer Student A's questions about the people (1–4) above.
- Ask Student A *only* yes/no questions about the people (5–8) below and write the names in the blanks next to the places.

ASK

5 Amy   6 Bill   7 Cheri and Dan   8 (Student A)

Example

| Student A | Was Eve at the park yesterday? |
| Student B | No, she wasn't. |

| Student B | Were Cheri and Dan at home yesterday? |
| Student A | Yes, they were. |

Exercise 3   Work with everyone.

Memo
- In Exercise 3, don't ask yes/no questions.
- Try to finish first!

Walk around the classroom and ask different classmates *where* they were yesterday. Write each classmate's name next to the place. Continue until every blank has a name.

Example

| Student A | Where were you yesterday? |
| Student C | I was at the park. |

name(s)

name(s)

name(s)

name(s)

name(s)

name(s)

name(s)

name(s)

name(s)

name(s)

name(s)

name(s)

Student A, turn to page 68

Student B

Speaking task two

Exercise 1

Take turns with Student A asking and answering questions about what the people below did last weekend. For the empty boxes, find out the following information and write it in one or two sentences: **(1)** *what* they did, **(2)** *when* they did it, **(3)** *where* they did it, **(4)** *who* they did it with and **(5)** *how long* they did it.

> **Memo**
>
> Answer each question separately. Don't read the sentence to Student A.

Example

Student B What did Naoko do last weekend?	**Student B** Where did she play?
Student A She played tennis.	**Student A** She played at the park.

Paul

Paul went swimming at the beach with his cousin on Saturday. They were at the beach all day, for about seven hours.

Naoko

Monica

Antonio

Antonio worked out at the sports club for about two hours on Saturday afternoon. He worked out with his brother.

Luke and Sara

Luke and Sara played cards at their friend's house on Sunday night. They played cards with their friends for about four hours.

Lina and Marco

Exercise 2

Ask Student A similar questions about what he or she did last weekend. Write all the information in one or two sentences.

> **Memo**
>
> Take turns asking and answering questions.

Student A

Speaking task one

Exercise 1   Work alone.

Fill in *any* ten boxes in Chart B using the actions in the pictures below (or on pages 71 or 74). Fill in the other five boxes with a question mark (**?**).

> **Memo**
> • Write notes in the boxes, not sentences.
> • Use each action only one time.

Example

play cards

Chart B	Sarah	Harold	Jean and Barry	Clara	Mia and Naomi
Saturday morning					
Saturday afternoon					
Saturday evening					

Exercise 2   Work with a partner.

Look at Chart A on page 72 and ask Student A what the people in Chart A are going to do. Fill in Chart A. When you have finished, look at Chart B above and answer Student A's questions about the people.

> **Memo**
> **?** = "I don't know."

Example

Student A	What's Sarah going to do Saturday morning?		**Student A**	What are Jean and Barry going to do Saturday afternoon?
Student B	She's going to play tennis.		**Student B**	I don't know.

Exercise 3   Work with everyone.

Walk around the classroom, and ask and answer questions. Find answers for all the boxes with a question mark (**?**) in Chart A and Chart B.

Student A, turn to page 77

Student B

Speaking task one

Speak to Student A on the phone twelve times. Ask to speak to *each* of the twelve people below. Listen to your partner's reply and check (✓) the correct box each time.

Example

| **Student B** | Could I speak to Larry? |
| **Student A** | Sure, just a moment. |

Larry — in ✓ / out / wrong #

Memo

Ask for people in different ways.

Anna — in / out / wrong #

Barry — in / out / wrong #

Charlie — in / out / wrong #

Donna — in / out / wrong #

Ed — in / out / wrong #

Fran — in / out / wrong #

Gary — in / out / wrong #

Helen — in / out / wrong #

Iris — in / out / wrong #

Jeff — in / out / wrong #

Kris — in / out / wrong #

Larry — in / out / wrong #

Example

| **Student B** | May I speak to Fran, please? |
| **Student A** | Speaking. |

| **Student B** | Could I speak to Helen? |
| **Student A** | Sorry, she's out right now. |

| **Student B** | Can I speak to Ed? |
| **Student A** | Sure, just a moment. |

| **Student B** | May I speak to Charlie? |
| **Student A** | I'm sorry. You have the wrong number. |

Memo

Change roles as Student A and Student B, and do the exercise again.

Player, turn to page 84

Caller

Language game   Play this game with two to four "players" and one "caller."

Before you begin the game, number the questions and answers below from 1 to 24 in *random order* (all mixed up).

The players will take turns choosing two numbers. Listen for the first number and read the first sentence. Listen for the second number, read the second sentence and say if it matches the first sentence or not.*
After that, the next player chooses.

Continue until all the questions and answers are matched. The player with the most matches wins!

*You can also ask the players if it is a match before you tell them.

> **Memo**
> - Read each sentence slowly, once or twice.
> - Read both of the sentences before you say, "They match!" or "They don't match!"

Example

Player A	Number 7.		**Player B**	Number 20.
Caller	"Did you do the homework?"		**Caller**	"No, I didn't. I forgot."
Player A	Number 12.		**Player B**	Number 7.
Caller	"They went to Italy." They don't match!		**Caller**	"Did you do the homework?" They match!

Question	Answer
( ) Was he at school yesterday?	( ) No, he was sick, so he stayed at home.
( ) What did they do last summer?	( ) They went to Italy.
( ) What did you and Bill do after school?	( ) We went to the supermarket.
( ) When did you go skiing?	( ) I went last January.
( ) Did you do the homework?	( ) No, I didn't. I forgot.
( ) How often do you work out?	( ) Oh, about three times a week.
( ) Where do you usually study?	( ) At the library.
( ) Are they going to take a bus?	( ) No, they're going to drive.
( ) When are they going to fly to Hawaii?	( ) They're going to leave next month.
( ) What's she going to do on Sunday?	( ) She's going to go shopping at the mall.
( ) Hello, is John there?	( ) Yes, he is. Just a moment.
( ) Hello, is Mary there?	( ) No, she's out right now.

Self-study exercise

Listen to each conversation and put the lines in order.

Conversation one ▣ 1

☐ I'm not sure. Is that a business address?

☐ Great, thanks.

☐ No, it's an apartment building called Garden Towers.

☐ Excuse me, do you know where 40-15 East 13th Street is?

☐ Oh, sure, that's around the corner, on the right.

Conversation two ▣ 2

☐ Is this area code 845?

☐ Oh, sorry. I misdialed.

☐ Hello. May I speak to John Chang?

☐ Is this 753-2446?

☐ No problem.

☐ I'm sorry, you have the wrong number.

☐ Yes, it is, but there is no John Chang here.

☐ No, it's not. It's 815.

Conversation three ▣ 3

☐ C-H-E-O-N.

☐ 096-82-8489.

☐ Could I have your name, please?

☐ OK ... and could you tell me your social security number?

☐ How do you spell your last name?

☐ OK, just a minute.

☐ Mia Cheon.

Self-study exercises

Exercise 1 4

Listen to the conversation and write "T" (true) or "F" (false) next to each sentence. Then listen again and rewrite the false sentences to make them true.

	It is the woman's first time in traffic court.	
	The woman is not nervous.	
	The man speaks Chinese.	
	The woman speaks Italian.	
	The woman is from Ecuador.	
	The man is from Japan.	
	The man lives in the country.	
	The woman lives in the suburbs.	
	The man gets a lot of parking tickets.	
	The woman gets some parking tickets.	

Exercise 2 5

Rewrite these sentences from the conversation in the correct order. Then listen again and check your answers.

> **Memo**
> Add punctuation and use capital letters where necessary.

1   language / do / what / you speak

_____

2   the judge / maybe / speaks Spanish

_____

3   English and Italian / he speaks / said / someone

_____

4   never / get / parking tickets / I

_____

107

 **Self-study exercises**

Exercise 1 6

Listen to the sentences. Find the differences.

1 It's in the file cabinet.

2 It's in the briefcase, on the desk.

3 It's next to the camera, on the left.

4 It's on the wall, on the right, under the fish tank.

5 They're on the wall, next to the file cabinet.

6 It's on the wall, near the window, on the left.

7 It's on the desk, behind the camera and the fax machine.

8 They're in the desk, next to the briefcase.

9 It's in the middle of the board, in front of the fax machine.

10 It's on the desk, behind the bookcase.

> **Memo**
> - Cross out (✗) the words that don't match and write in the correct words.
> - Some of the sentences don't contain any differences.

Exercise 2 7

Listen to the sentences. Fill in the missing words.

1 The CD player is next to the _____ cabinet.

2 The _____ are next to the briefcase, on the right.

3 The newspaper is on the briefcase, in the _____

4 The _____ are on the floor, behind the file cabinet.

5 The clock is on the _____ , next to the window, on the right.

6 The calculator is in front of the fax machine, in the _____ of the desk.

7 The _____ is over the fish tank, on the wall.

8 The _____ are on the desk, between the camera and the fax machine.

9 The _____ is under the desk, next to the scissors.

10 The _____ is on the desk, next to the camera.

> **Memo**
> Add punctuation and use capital letters where necessary.

108

4 Self-study exercises

Exercise 1 8

Listen to the conversation and check (✓) the four questions that *can* be answered. Then listen again and write the answers to the four questions.

☐ What is Megan playing with?

☐ What game are Erica and Nicky playing?

☐ What is Bob watching on TV?

☐ What is Mary talking about?

☐ Who is Susan's mother feeding?

☐ What is Susan's brother doing?

Exercise 2 9

Rewrite these sentences from the conversation in the correct order. Then listen and check your answers.

Memo

Add punctuation and use capital letters where necessary.

1 what / all that / is / noise

_____

2 your sister / came over / so / Mary

_____

3 is talking / Mary / your mother / with

_____

4 Dad's taking / in his favorite armchair / a nap

_____

 **Self-study exercises**

Exercise 1   10

Listen to the sentences. Find the differences.

1 She's a doctor.

2 I walk at night.

3 Peter works in a restroom.

4 I have a uniform.

5 Lisa and Bill work in the cinema.

6 Diane has a bus.

7 They go to work by taxi.

8 Mr. Ford teaches French.

Exercise 2   11

Listen to the sentences. Fill in the missing words.

1 He always works _____

2 He always wears a _____ at work.

3 He _____ a lot at work.

4 He _____ outdoors.

5 He usually _____ to customers.

6 He usually sits _____ at work.

7 He usually works _____

8 He sometimes works all _____

9 He works in his _____

10 He _____ a lot of things at work.

Self-study exercise

Listen to the conversations (1–3) and choose the best answer to each question.

Conversation one (Uncle Gregory and Joey) 12

1 What do Uncle Gregory and Joey mainly talk about?

   a. Joey's brother

   b. Joey's hobbies

   c. Joey's favorite sport

   d. Joey's school

2 What do Uncle Gregory and Joey decide to do together?

   a. watch TV

   b. go bowling

   c. go to the beach

   d. see a movie

Conversation two (Amy and Mom) 13

1 What are Amy's hobbies?

   a. reading and going to the library

   b. staying in bed and going to the cafeteria

   c. shopping and jogging

   d. going to the mall and spending time alone

2 What does Amy's roommate like to read?

   a. magazines

   b. newspapers

   c. poetry

   d. novels

Conversation three (Frank and Sheri) 14

1 Why doesn't Sheri like to go dancing?

   a. It's boring.

   b. It's too expensive.

   c. It's too loud and too crowded.

   d. It's too difficult and too tiring.

2 When does Sheri take photographs?

   a. every Monday

   b. every Friday

   c. every Saturday

   d. every Sunday

 **Self-study exercises**

Exercise 1 15

Listen to the conversation and check (✓) the four questions that *can* be answered. Then listen again and write the answers to the four questions.

Where is the tent?

What color is the tent?

How many pots and pans do John and Denise have?

Who has the compass?

Who has the sleeping bags?

Why is John's backpack so heavy?

Exercise 2 16

Rewrite these sentences from the conversation in the correct order. Then listen and check your answers.

> **Memo**
>
> Add punctuation and use capital letters where necessary.

1 do / the tent / have / we

_____

2 the / how / insect spray / about

_____

3 the sleeping bags / I / and / the canteen / have

_____

4 I / everything / think / well / that's

_____

 **Self-study exercise**

Listen to each conversation and put the lines in order.

Conversation one 🔽 17

☐ OK, I'll take two. And do you have nail clippers?

☐ Here you are. The aspirin is two forty-nine a bottle and the Band-Aids are three fifty a box.

☐ Well, I don't need it right now. I'll just take these.

☐ Excuse me, I'm looking for a toothbrush.

☐ Sure, right here. They're a dollar twenty-five.

☐ Oh, no, they're too big. Let's see, I also need aspirin and Band-Aids.

☐ It's four seventy-five.

☐ Yes, we do, over there. Ninety-nine cents.

☐ OK. Oh, how much is this baby powder?

Conversation two 🔽 18

☐ That's apple pie. It's six seventy-five.

☐ It's twelve fifty.

☐ I'll take a dozen doughnuts and a half pound of cookies.

☐ OK, the doughnuts are four fifty a dozen, and the cookies are eight dollars a pound.

☐ Excuse me, what kind of pie is that?

☐ Oh, that's too expensive. How about these cookies, and those doughnuts over there?

☐ Oh, sorry, I don't like apple. Can I have two loaves of French bread, please?

☐ OK, and how much is that large fruitcake?

☐ Sure, they're one twenty-nine a loaf.

Self-study exercises

Exercise 1

Listen to the conversations (1–5) and write "T" (true) or "F" (false) next to each sentence.

Conversation one 📥 19

☐ Jenny was at Alan's barbecue.

☐ Jenny's sister arrived late.

Conversation two 📥 20

☐ Bruce was with his family.

☐ Bruce played basketball with his sons.

Conversation three 📥 21

☐ Colin and Lisa were not at Alan's barbecue.

☐ Colin and Lisa went to see a movie.

Conversation four 📥 22

☐ Ed was at Alan's barbecue.

☐ Ed got a haircut.

Conversation five 📥 23

☐ Fern was sick.

☐ Fern went to work.

Exercise 2

Rewrite the false sentences to make them true.

12 Self-study exercise

 24

Listen to the conversation and choose the best answer to each question.

1 What is this conversation mainly about?

- **a.** Darren's shoes
- **b.** Darren's shopping
- **c.** Darren's dinner
- **d.** Darren's jeans

2 Where did Darren buy his jeans?

- **a.** at the mall
- **b.** at the market
- **c.** at a department store
- **d.** at a garage sale

3 What did Darren want to buy at the sports shop?

- **a.** weights
- **b.** sneakers
- **c.** a T-shirt
- **d.** a basketball

4 What kind of CD did Darren buy?

- **a.** pop
- **b.** classical
- **c.** heavy metal
- **d.** jazz

5 What is on the T-shirt?

- **a.** a dragon
- **b.** a tiger
- **c.** a picture of Darren
- **d.** a heavy metal band

6 Where did Darren leave the food?

- **a.** at a restaurant
- **b.** at the sports shop
- **c.** in a taxi
- **d.** on the subway

www.fifty-fifty-series.com

Self-study exercise

Listen to each conversation and put the lines in order.

Conversation one 25

I'm going to go swimming.

So am I!

Me, too. It's going to be great!

What are you going to do tomorrow morning, Bren?

I'm going to go hiking.

Oh. I'm going to go horseback riding.

Oh, really? What are you going to do in the evening?

What about tomorrow afternoon, Abel?

I'm going to see the fireworks.

Conversation two 26

I'm going to go water skiing.

I think so. I don't know. Um, what are you going to do?

Oh, yeah? So am I.

Are you going to go to the disco tomorrow evening?

OK, I'll see you there. It's going to be fun.

No, I'm not. Are you?

Well, Chad, what are you going to do tomorrow morning?

Conversation three 27

So am I!

Oh, I don't think so, Eli. But what are you going to do tomorrow evening?

I'm going to see a movie.

Great! This is going to be a great vacation.

Yeah, me too. I'll meet you at the tennis courts.

I'm going to play tennis tomorrow morning, Fay. How about you?

Are you going to go to the sauna after lunch?

Self-study exercises

Exercise 1

Memo

Cross out (✗) the words that don't match the conversation and write in the correct words.

Listen to the conversations (1 and 2). Find the differences in each conversation below.

Conversation one 28

Woman 1	Hello?
Woman 2	Hello. Could I speak to Sarah, please?
Woman 1	Sorry, she's out right now.
Woman 2	Oh, OK. I'll try again later.
Woman 1	OK, goodbye.
Woman 2	Bye.

Coversation two 29

Woman	Hello.
Man	Hello. Is Della home?
Woman	Della? Sorry, you have the wrong number.
Man	Oh, sorry.
Woman	That's all right.

Exercise 2

Memo

Add punctuation and use capital letters where necessary.

Listen to the conversations (3 and 4). Fill in the missing words.

Conversation three ⬇ 30

Man	Hello.
Woman	Hello. Could I _____ to Jim, please?
Man	_____ I ask who's calling?
Woman	My name is Gina Lombardi. I'm an _____ friend.
Man	Sure, hold on just a _____ , please.
Woman	OK, thanks.

Conversation four ⬇ 31

Man 1	Hello?
Man 2	Hello. May I speak to Mike, _____
Man 1	Speaking.
Man 2	Mike, it's Dave Zuber. How's _____
Man 1	Hi, Dave! _____ , I can't talk right now. Can I call you _____ later?
Man 2	Sure, no _____ Talk to you later. Bye.
Man 1	Bye.

SELF-STUDY EXERCISES ANSWER KEY

UNIT ❶

Conversation one	Conversation two	Conversation three
2	5	4
5	7	6
3	1	1
1	3	5
4	8	3
	2	7
	4	2
	6	

UNIT ❷

Exercise 1

- [T / **F**] The woman is nervous.
- [T / **F**] The woman speaks Spanish.
- [T / **F**] The man is from Taiwan.
- [T / **F**] The man lives in the city.
- [**T** / F]
- [**T** / F]
- [T / **F**] The woman never gets parking tickets.

Exercise 2

1 What language do you speak?
2 Maybe the judge speaks Spanish.
3 Someone said he speaks English and Italian.
4 I never get parking tickets.

UNIT ❸

Exercise 1

1 It's ~~in~~ the file cabinet.   on
2 It's in the briefcase, on the desk.
3 ~~It's~~ next to the camera, on the left.   They're
4 It's on the wall, on the right, ~~under~~ the fish tank.   over
5 They're on the ~~wall~~, next to the file cabinet.   floor
6 It's on the wall, ~~near~~ the window, on the left.   next to
7 It's on the desk, ~~behind~~ the camera and the fax machine.   between
8 They're ~~in~~ the desk, next to the briefcase.   on
9 It's in the middle of the ~~board~~, in front of the fax machine.   desk
10 It's on the desk, behind the ~~bookcase~~.   briefcase

Exercise 2

1	file	6	middle
2	scissors	7	calendar
3	desk.	8	keys
4	weights	9	lamp
5	wall	10	watch

UNIT ❹

Exercise 1

- [✓] Megan is playing with the dog.
- [ ]
- [✓] Bob is watching a basketball game.
- [ ]
- [✓] Susan's mother is feeding Megan.
- [✓] Susan's brother is changing a light bulb.

Exercise 2

1 What is all that noise?
2 So, your sister Mary came over?
3 Mary is talking with your mother.
4 Dad's taking a nap in his favorite armchair.

UNIT ❻

Exercise 1

1 ~~She's~~ a doctor.   Sue's
2 I ~~walk~~ at night.   work
3 Peter works in a ~~restroom~~.   restaurant
4 I ~~have~~ a uniform.   wear
5 Lisa and Bill work in the ~~cinema~~.   city
6 Diane ~~has~~ a bus.   drives
7 They ~~go~~ to work by taxi.   get
8 Mr. ~~Ford~~ teaches French.   Hall

Exercise 2

1	indoors.	6	down
2	uniform	7	alone.
3	walks	8	night.
4	works	9	office.
5	talks	10	carries

UNIT ❼

Conversation one

1 b   2 d

Conversation two

1 c   2 a

Conversation three

1 c   2 d

UNIT 8

Exercise 1

- ☑ The tent is in John's backpack.
- ☐
- ☐
- ☑ Denise has the compass.
- ☑ John has the sleeping bags.
- ☑ Because he has all of Denise's guidebooks.

Exercise 2

1 Do we have the tent?
2 How about the insect spray?
3 I have the sleeping bags and the canteen.
4 Well, I think that's everything.

UNIT 9

Conversation one	Conversation two
3	2
6	6
9	9
1	8
2	1
5	7
8	3
4	5
7	4

UNIT 11

Conversation one
- F Jenny was not at Alan's barbecue.
- T

Conversation two
- T
- F Bruce played soccer with his sons.

Conversation three
- T
- F Colin and Lisa went shopping.

Conversation four
- F Ed was not at Alan's barbecue.
- T

Conversation five
- T
- F Fern stayed in bed all day.

UNIT 12

1	b	2	a	3	b
4	c	5	a	6	d

UNIT 13

Conversation one	Conversation two	Conversation three
2	2	6
6	7	4
9	3	5
1	5	7
5	4	2
3	6	1
7	1	3
4		
8		

UNIT 14

Exercise 1

Conversation one

Woman 1 Hello?
Woman 2 Hello. ~~Could~~ I speak to Sarah, please?   Can
Woman 1 Sorry, she's ~~out~~ right now.   not in
Woman 2 Oh, OK. I'll ~~try~~ again later.   call
Woman 1 OK, ~~goodbye~~.   bye
Woman 2 Bye.

Conversation two

Woman Hello.
Man Hello. Is Della ~~home~~?   there
Woman Della? ~~Sorry~~, you have the wrong   I'm sorry
number.
Man Oh, sorry.
Woman That's ~~all right~~.   OK

Exercise 2

Conversation three

Man Hello.
Woman Hello. Could I <u>speak</u> to Jim, please?
Man <u>May</u> I ask who's calling?
Woman My name is Gina Lombardi. I'm an <u>old</u> friend.
Man Sure, hold on just a <u>moment</u> , please.
Woman OK, thanks.

Conversation four

Man 1 Hello?
Man 2 Hello. May I speak to Mike, <u>please?</u>
Man 1 Speaking.
Man 2 Mike, it's Dave Zuber. How's <u>everything?</u>
Man 1 Hi, Dave! <u>Listen</u> , I can't talk right now. Can I
call you <u>back</u> later?
Man 2 Sure, no <u>problem.</u> Talk to you later. Bye.
Man 1 Bye.

Audio Script

Getting Started

Listening task, page 3

Exercise one 2

1 Are we late?
2 Where's the classroom?
3 Do you have the textbook?
4 When does class begin?
5 Is he the teacher?
6 Where are all the students?
7 Is it a large class?
8 Are you in class 3A?

Exercise two 3

Boy	Excuse me, is this the reading class?
Girl	Yes, it is. Are you a new student?
Boy	Yes, I am. I really like reading.
Girl	Me, too. Where do you live?
Boy	I live in Bayview.
Girl	Oh, I live in Hillside.
Boy	Is that near the school?
Girl	Yes, it is. I walk to school.
Boy	I take a bus.
Girl	Are you in the afternoon writing class?
Boy	Yes, I am. Are you?
Girl	Yeah, and it's *not* an easy class.

Unit 1

Listening task, page 7

Exercises one and two

Conversation one 5

Woman	Excuse me, do you know where 40-15 East 13th Street is?
Man	I'm not sure. Is that a business address?
Woman	No, it's an apartment building called Garden Towers.
Man	Oh, sure, that's around the corner, on the right.
Woman	Great, thanks.

Conversation two 6

Man	Hello. May I speak to John Chang?
Woman	I'm sorry, you have the wrong number.
Man	Is this 753-2446?
Woman	Yes, it is, but there is no John Chang here.

Man	Is this area code 845?
Woman	No, it's not. It's 815.
Man	Oh, sorry. I misdialed.
Woman	No problem.

Conversation three 7

Man	Could I have your name, please?
Woman	Mia Cheon.
Man	How do you spell your last name?
Woman	C-H-E-O-N.
Man	OK ... and could you tell me your social security number?
Woman	096-82-8489.
Man	OK, just a minute.

Unit 2

Listening task, page 12

Exercise one 9–11

1 My name is Meena. I speak Hindi. I'm from India. I live in New Delhi.

2 His name is Bernard. He lives in Geneva. He's from Switzerland. He speaks French.

3 My name is Roberto, and her name is Paola. We're from Brazil. We speak Portuguese. We live in Rio de Janeiro.

Exercise two 12

Man	Is this your first time in a traffic court?
Woman	Yes, it is. I'm nervous. I only speak English a little.
Man	Really? Me, too. I speak Chinese. What language do you speak?
Woman	I speak Spanish.
Man	Maybe the judge speaks Spanish.
Woman	No, he doesn't. Someone said he speaks English and Italian.
Man	Don't worry. You speak English well.
Woman	No, no, only a little. I am from Ecuador.
Man	I'm from Taiwan.
Woman	Are you nervous?
Man	No, I'm not. I live in the city. I get a lot of parking tickets.
Woman	I live in the suburbs. I never get parking tickets.

Listening task, page 18

Exercise one 14

1 The scissors are on the desk, next to the briefcase.
2 The keys are next to the camera, on the left.
3 The weights are on the floor, next to the file cabinet.
4 The lamp is on the desk, behind the briefcase.
5 The calendar is on the wall, on the right, over the fish tank.
6 The calculator is in the middle of the desk, in front of the fax machine.
7 The CD player is on the file cabinet.
8 The clock is on the wall, next to the window, on the left.
9 The newspaper is in the briefcase, on the desk.
10 The watch is on the desk, between the camera and the fax machine.

Exercise two 15

1 It's on the file cabinet.
2 It's in the briefcase, on the desk.
3 They're next to the camera, on the left.
4 It's on the wall, on the right, over the fish tank.
5 They're on the floor, next to the file cabinet.
6 It's on the wall, next to the window, on the left.
7 It's on the desk, between the camera and the fax machine.
8 They're on the desk, next to the briefcase.
9 It's in the middle of the desk, in front of the fax machine.
10 It's on the desk, behind the briefcase.

Exercise three 16

1 The CD player is next to the file cabinet.
2 The scissors are next to the briefcase, on the right.
3 The newspaper is on the briefcase, in the desk.
4 The weights are on the floor, behind the file cabinet.
5 The clock is on the wall, next to the window, on the right.
6 The calculator is in front of the fax machine, in the middle of the desk.
7 The calendar is over the fish tank, on the wall.
8 The keys are on the desk, between the camera and the fax machine.
9 The lamp is under the desk, next to the scissors.
10 The watch is on the desk, next to the camera.

Listening task, page 24

Exercise one 18

Susan	Hello?
Paul	Hi, Susan. *What* is all that noise? How's the baby?
Susan	Oh, hi, Paul. Megan's fine. She's playing with the dog.
Paul	Who's yelling?
Susan	Oh, that's Erica and Nicky. They're playing together.
Paul	Nicky? So, your sister Mary came over?
Susan	Yeah, Bob came, too. He's watching a basketball game on TV. Mary is talking with your mother.
Paul	My mother? Are Mom and Dad there, too?
Susan	Uh-huh. Dad's taking a nap in his favorite armchair. My mother's here, too. She's feeding Megan.
Paul	What's breaking? What *is* that?
Susan	I don't know. Just a minute. Oh, that's Jimmy. He's changing a light bulb.
Paul	Oh, your brother is there, too.

Exercise two 19

1 Johnny is playing with Nicky.
2 The baby is playing with the cat.
3 Nicky is breaking a light bulb.
4 Mary is talking with Paul's mother.
5 Dad is taking a nap on the couch.
6 Susan is talking with Paul's father.
7 Susan's mother is feeding the dog.
8 Bob is watching a movie on TV.

UNIT 5

Listening task, page 29

Exercises one and two

Conversation one 20

Mother	What are you doing, Marcus?
Son	I'm looking for Thailand.
Mother	Thailand?
Son	Yeah, those new neighbors across the street are from Thailand.
Mother	Oh, really? Do they speak English?
Son	Yeah, they speak English a little. How do you spell Thailand?
Mother	T-H-A-I-L-A-N-D. It's below China.

Conversation two

Woman	Hold it!
Man	What?
Woman	Don't move!
Man	What's wrong?
Woman	What are you doing in this building?
Man	I'm working late.
Woman	Oh? Where's your ID card?
Man	It's in my briefcase, in my wallet.

Conversation three

Man	How do you spell your first name, Miss Tomei?
Woman	Y-O-S-H-I-E.
Man	And you are from Japan, Yoshi?
Woman	I'm sorry, that's "Yoshie." And yes, I'm from Japan.
Man	OK. Look at page ten. You are riding on a bus. You are sitting next to your son. He's crying. Please read from line twenty-three.
Woman	I'm sorry, but am I crying, too?
Man	No, *you're* not crying. Your *son* is crying. From line twenty-three, please.

Conversation four

Man	Oh, it's my turn. Well, my partner's name is Hilda. She's from Australia, and—
Woman	No, no, I am from *Austria*.
Man	Oh. OK, she's from Austria, and she speaks English, German and Flemish. She's—
Woman	No, I speak English, German and *French*.
Man	Oh, and French, not Flemish. OK. She's studying English because ... because ... um, I forget. Why *are* you in this class, Hilda?

UNIT 6

Listening task, pages 34 and 35

Exercises one and two

1   Sue's a doctor.
2   I work at night.
3   Peter works in a restaurant.
4   I wear a uniform.
5   Lisa and Bill work in the city.
6   Diane drives a bus.
7   They get to work by taxi.
8   Mr. Hall teaches French.

Exercise three

1   He always works indoors.
2   He always wears a uniform at work.

3   He walks a lot at work.
4   He works outdoors.
5   He usually talks to customers.
6   He usually sits down at work.
7   He usually works alone.
8   He sometimes works all night.
9   He works in his office.
10 He carries a lot of things at work.

Exercise four

1   I carry a lot of things at work. I walk a lot. I work on the street. I usually work alone.
2   I usually sit down at work. I sometimes work all night. I usually talk to customers. I work outdoors.
3   I sometimes work all night. I always work indoors. I usually work alone. I work in my office.
4   I work indoors. I always wear a uniform. I walk a lot. I usually carry a lot of things.

UNIT 7

Listening task, page 40

Exercises one and two

Conversation one

Uncle Gregory	So, what would you like to do while you're here, Joey?
Joey	I don't know, Uncle Gregory.
Uncle Gregory	Well, what do you usually do in your free time?
Joey	I like to watch TV ... every night.
Uncle Gregory	TV? Oh ... OK. What about sports?
Joey	Sports? Well, I like to go bowling sometimes. I go with my brother.
Uncle Gregory	Bowling? Oh. Well, do you like to go swimming? There's a great beach near here.
Joey	I go swimming at school, but I don't really like it.
Uncle Gregory	Oh, I see. Hmm. Do you like to go to the movies?
Joey	Sure. I sometimes go on Saturday.
Uncle Gregory	Great! We can go tomorrow night.
Joey	OK.

Conversation two

Amy	I have a new roommate at school, Mom.
Mom	Oh, that's nice, Amy. Do you two do things together?
Amy	No, not at all. You know, I like going shopping at the mall on the weekends, but she likes to go to the library.

Mom	The library? Well, what does she like to do in her free time?
Amy	She likes to read magazines. She reads in bed, she reads in the cafeteria ... oh yeah! She goes jogging in the morning.
Mom	Well, *you* like to go jogging, don't you?
Amy	Yeah, but she likes to go jogging *alone*.
Mom	Oh.
Amy	Yeah. She's a lot of fun.

Conversation three

Frank	Hey, Sheri, do you ever go to the movies?
Sheri	Not often. I don't really like going to the movies, Frank.
Frank	No? Well, do you like to go dancing?
Sheri	Sorry. I never go. It's always too loud and too crowded.
Frank	Oh. Well, what *do* you like to do in your free time?
Sheri	I like taking photographs.
Frank	You take pictures, huh?
Sheri	Yep. Every Sunday I go to the mountains. I took those photos on the wall over there.
Frank	Those are *yours*, Sheri? They're ... they're really good.
Sheri	Thanks. I also paint. This is mine, on the wall here.
Frank	That painting is yours, too? Wow.
Sheri	So, what do you like to do in your free time, Frank?
Frank	Me? Well, I, um ... let me see ... I don't know ... maybe ... um ...

UNIT 8

Listening task, page 45

Exercises one and two

John	OK, now let's check everything before we leave. Do we have the tent?
Denise	Yes, John, you have that. It's in your backpack. And the maps ... oh, I have them.
John	How about the insect spray? Do you have it?
Denise	Yes, I do. Don't worry.
John	OK. I have the camping stove, and the pots and pans, but I don't have the forks and knives.
Denise	I have the forks and knives, *and* the mugs and plates.
John	What about the compass, Denise?
Denise	Yeah, I have that, and the flashlight.
John	Good. I have the sleeping bags and the canteen. And you have the umbrellas, right?

Denise	Yeah. Well, I think that's everything.
John	Oh! My backpack is really heavy!
Denise	Oh, yeah, sorry. You have all my guidebooks.
John	Guidebooks? What guidebooks?

UNIT 9

Listening task, page 50

Exercises one and two

Conversation one

Woman	Excuse me, I'm looking for a toothbrush.
Man	Sure, right here. They're a dollar twenty-five.
Woman	OK, I'll take two. And do you have nail clippers?
Man	Yes, we do, over there. Ninety-nine cents.
Woman	Oh, no, they're too big. Let's see, I also need aspirin and Band-Aids.
Man	Here you are. The aspirin is two forty-nine a bottle and the Band-Aids are three fifty a box.
Woman	OK. Oh, how much is this baby powder?
Man	It's four seventy-five.
Woman	Well, I don't need it right now. I'll just take these.

Conversation two

Man	Excuse me, what kind of pie is that?
Woman	That's apple pie. It's six seventy-five.
Man	Oh, sorry, I don't like apple. Can I have two loaves of French bread, please?
Woman	Sure, they're one twenty-nine a loaf.
Man	OK, and how much is that large fruitcake?
Woman	It's twelve fifty.
Man	Oh, that's too expensive. How about these cookies, and those doughnuts over there?
Woman	OK, the doughnuts are four fifty a dozen, and the cookies are eight dollars a pound.
Man	I'll take a dozen doughnuts and a half pound of cookies.

Conversation three

Man	Hi, I'm looking for a battery for this camera.
Woman	Sure, we have those. They're nine ninety-five each.
Man	OK, I'll take two. Do you have a lens cap for this camera, too?
Woman	Yes, right here. It's only two dollars and fifty cents.
Man	Fine.

Woman	How about a memory card? They're on sale, nineteen ninety-eight or two for thirty-five dollars.
Man	Thanks, but I don't need a memory card right now. How much are those photo albums?
Woman	They're also on sale, eight dollars each.
Man	Yeah, that's not expensive, but I don't like the color.

UNIT

Listening task, page 55

Exercises one and two

Conversation one

Martin	Is Saturday OK?
Adriana	I'm sorry, Martin, but I go shopping every Saturday.
Martin	How about Sunday?
Adriana	I play tennis Sunday morning and have a piano lesson in the afternoon. How about a weekday?
Martin	I work part time after school every day.
Adriana	So, when can we work on our assignment?
Martin	How about before class on Monday and Wednesday?
Adriana	OK! Good, let's meet here on Monday at eight o'clock.

Conversation two

Father	What does your new boyfriend do?
Daughter	I want to surprise you, Dad. He's coming here now, on his way to work.
Father	He works at night?
Daughter	Well, he usually works in the evening, but on weekends he works in the afternoon, too.
Father	He works on Saturday and Sunday? Is he a salesman?
Daughter	No, he isn't a salesman. Wait till you see him!
Father	See him? Does he wear a uniform or something?
Daughter	No, he doesn't wear a uniform, but ...
Father	But what?

Conversation three

Husband	Can we go now, Brenda?
Wife	No, I'm looking for a sweater.
Husband	A sweater? You have a dozen sweaters.
Wife	I don't have a yellow sweater.
Husband	Oh. You want a yellow sweater.

Wife	That's right. Ooh, how much are those boots?
Husband	These? They're too expensive.
Wife	No, they're not. I have a credit card. Oh, look at this dress! How much is this?

Conversation four

Allison	Where's Kathy, George?
George	She's picking up the kids.
Allison	Oh, do you have two cars now, George?
George	Yes, Allison, we have a new minivan.
Allison	Oh? That's nice for the children, I guess … but I love my Mercedes.
George	I know, Allison. You have four.
Allison	Well, yes, but one is mine, one is my husband's, one is my daughter's and—
George	I know, one is for family trips with your dog.
Allison	Well, sometimes little Babette is messy in the car.

UNIT 11

Listening task, page 60

Exercises one and two

Conversation one

Alan	Hi, Jenny. Where were you yesterday?
Jenny	I picked up my sister. Her flight was six hours late! It was terrible!
Alan	Oh. Sorry you missed my barbecue.

Conversation two

| Alan | Where was Bruce yesterday? |
| Jenny | Bruce? He was with his family at the park. He played soccer with his sons. |

Conversation three

| Betsy | Were Colin and Lisa at Alan's barbecue yesterday? |
| Jenny | No, they weren't. They went shopping. |

Conversation four

| Jenny | Was Ed at the barbecue? |
| Betsy | No, he wasn't. He got a haircut. |

Conversation five

Alan	Hi, Fern.
Fern	Oh, hi, Alan.
Alan	Where were you yesterday?
Fern	I was sick. I stayed in bed all day.
Alan	Oh, sorry to hear that.

Conversation six

Alan	Gina! Where were you and Tom yesterday?
Gina	Oh, Alan, it was so hot! We went swimming. So, how was your barbecue?
Alan	Well, it was … quiet.

UNIT 12

Listening task, page 66

Exercises one and two

Darren	Julia, I'm home!
Julia	Did you get the food for dinner?
Darren	Yeah, and I got some other things, too. Look, I bought these jeans at that new shop in the mall.
Julia	Are they the right size?
Darren	Sure, I tried them on. I went to the sports shop, too. They had a sale on sneakers, but they didn't have my size.
Julia	Darren, you have four pairs of sneakers. How about the food?
Darren	Yeah, wait a minute. I got a couple of paperbacks, some toothpaste and … oh yeah, I bought this CD for you.
Julia	"Heavy Metal Greatest Hits"? Darren, I hate heavy metal!
Darren	Well, we can give it to your mother for her birthday. Let's see, I wanted to get some batteries for the radio, but I forgot the size. Oh, and I picked up this T-shirt for you. That's a great dragon, isn't it?
Julia	Oh, thanks, Darren, but, well, I don't know. So, where's the food?
Darren	It's … huh? Oh, no! I left it on the subway.
Julia	You left the food on the subway!
Darren	Yeah, sorry. Listen, let's go out to eat. You can wear the dragon T-shirt.
Julia	Great, Darren, that's great.

UNIT 13

Listening task, page 71

Exercises one and two

Conversation one

Abel	What are you going to do tomorrow morning, Bren?
Bren	I'm going to go swimming.
Abel	Oh. I'm going to go horseback riding.
Bren	What about tomorrow afternoon, Abel?

Abel	I'm going to go hiking.
Bren	So am I!
Abel	Oh, really? What are you going to do in the evening?
Bren	I'm going to see the fireworks.
Abel	Me, too. It's going to be great!

Conversation two

Dori	Well, Chad, what are you going to do tomorrow morning?
Chad	I'm going to go water skiing.
Dori	Oh, yeah? So am I.
Chad	OK, I'll see you there. It's going to be fun.
Dori	Are you going to go to the disco tomorrow evening?
Chad	No, I'm not. Are you?
Dori	I think so. I don't know. Um, what are you going to do?

Conversation three

Eli	I'm going to play tennis tomorrow morning, Fay. How about you?
Fay	Yeah, me too. I'll meet you at the tennis courts.
Eli	Are you going to go to the sauna after lunch?
Fay	Oh, I don't think so, Eli. But what are you going to do tomorrow evening?
Eli	I'm going to see a movie.
Fay	So am I!
Eli	Great! This is going to be a great vacation.

UNIT 14

Listening task, page 76

Exercises one, two and three

Conversation one

Woman 1	Hello?
Woman 2	Hello. Can I speak to Sarah, please?
Woman 1	Sorry, she's not in right now.
Woman 2	Oh, OK. I'll call again later.
Woman 1	OK, bye.
Woman 2	Bye.

Conversation two

Woman	Hello.
Man	Hello. Is Della there?
Woman	Della? I'm sorry, you have the wrong number.
Man	Oh, sorry.
Woman	That's OK.

Conversation three

Man	Hello.
Woman	Hello. Could I speak to Jim, please?
Man	May I ask who's calling?
Woman	My name is Gina Lombardi. I'm an old friend.
Man	Sure, hold on just a moment, please.
Woman	OK, thanks.

Conversation four

Man 1	Hello?
Man 2	Hello. May I speak to Mike, please?
Man 1	Speaking.
Man 2	Mike, it's Dave Zuber. How's everything?
Man 1	Hi, Dave! Listen, I can't talk right now. Can I call you back later?
Man 2	Sure, no problem. Talk to you later. Bye.
Man 1	Bye.

UNIT ⑮

Listening task, page 81

Exercises one and two

Conversation one

Howard	Oh, Natalie! Hi, nice to see you.
Natalie	Hi, Howard. What are you doing?
Howard	Oh, just listening to music. What's up?
Natalie	Would you like to see my new computer?
Howard	Sure! When did you get it?
Natalie	I bought it yesterday. Come and see it.
Howard	OK, I'll be there in fifteen minutes. Thanks for calling.
Natalie	OK, bye.

Conversation two

Reiko	You have a nice house, Clayton.
Clayton	Thanks, Reiko. I spend a lot of time here. I usually stay at home in the evening.
Reiko	Do you like to watch TV?
Clayton	Yes, I do. I rent videos two or three times a week.
Reiko	Really? I like watching old movies on TV.
Clayton	Me, too. I have a new widescreen TV. It's really big. Would you like to see it?
Reiko	Sure.
Clayton	It's in here. Oh, yeah. I like listening to music, too.

Conversation three

Sam	So, what are you going to do today, Mabel?
Mabel	I'm going to go sightseeing, Sam.
Sam	Oh? What are you going to see?
Mabel	Well, I'm going to see Mount Everest, and then I'm going to look for Mount Fuji in Japan. How about you?
Sam	I'm going to play chess with my friend in Australia.
Mabel	Oh, that's nice.
Sam	The new computer is great, isn't it?
Mabel	Yes, it is, Sam. I just love surfing the Web.

Conversation four

Philip	Hello?
Mom	Philip? Where were you last weekend? I called three times.
Philip	I went skiing.
Mom	Oh? Who did you go with?
Philip	I went with Rob and Diane and Jeanie.
Mom	Did you have fun?
Philip	Yeah, it was great, but I broke my leg in the—
Mom	Oh, I knew it! Why didn't you call me?
Philip	I broke it this morning, Mom, in the shower. I called you, but you weren't at home.